Philanthropy, Innovation and Entrepreneurship

"It is essential that governments understand the impact of philanthropy and how it is changing. The insights in this book into the relationships between philanthropy, innovation and entrepreneurship need to be fully appreciated by policy makers."

—Baroness Mary Goudie, *House of Lords*

"Much of the adventure in science is supported by philanthropy. This book explains the important connections between philanthropy, innovation and entrepreneurship."

—Professor Stephen Caddick, *Director of Innovation, Wellcome Trust*

"Philanthropy supports the Arts and, as is shown in this book, it provides the means for them to be ever more adventurous, creative and innovative. Without this wonderful belief in our aspirations, we simply would not be in this position that we are today."

—Gus Christie, *Executive Chairman, Glyndebourne*

"At its most effective, philanthropy needs to be risk-taking, entrepreneurial and catalytic. This book clearly demonstrates how successful philanthropic outcomes depend on innovative ambitions."

—James Chen, *Philanthropist and Founder, Clearly*

Mark Dodgson · David Gann

Philanthropy, Innovation and Entrepreneurship

An Introduction

Mark Dodgson
The University of Queensland
St Lucia, QLD, Australia

David Gann
Imperial College London
London, UK

ISBN 978-3-030-38016-8   ISBN 978-3-030-38017-5   (eBook)
https://doi.org/10.1007/978-3-030-38017-5

This Palgrave Pivot imprint is published by the registered company Springer Nature Switzerland AG
The registered company address is: Gewerbestrasse 11, 6330 Cham, Switzerland

We dedicate this book to the generous donors to our home institutions, the University of Queensland and Imperial College London.

PREFACE

Between us we have been studying innovation and entrepreneurship for over 70 years and we have been interested in philanthropy for nearly as long. We have held numbers of positions in universities, businesses and artistic organizations that were either responsible for attracting or dispersing philanthropic funds. Through our research we have always been highly conscious of the close connections between philanthropy, innovation and entrepreneurship. Many successful entrepreneurs choose to direct wealth they create to philanthropic causes. Philanthropy supports innovation, and also seeks new ideas and approaches to assist deliver on its purpose.

An opportunity arose for us to focus our interest on philanthropy through an association with a charity: the Oxford Centre for the Study of Philanthropy, led by Professor Michael Earl and Stephen Barclay. Designed to raise the profile of research into philanthropy, the charity ran a very successful series of lectures on the subject, and gave us the opportunity for three years to interact with some of the leading thinkers on the subject. We are very grateful to Stephen and Michael, and to the others associated with the Centre, including Baroness Mary Goudie, Ashley Mitchell and Antonia Mitchell, for the opportunity they provided.

Many people have informed and guided our thinking on philanthropy, and we would like to thank Pascale Michaud, Lauren Friedman, Michael Mapstone, Anne Asha, Caroline Fiennes Howie Rush and Helen McCarthy. We are especially grateful to Kate Dodgson for helping us based on her work on innovation and humanitarian causes.

Mark Dodgson
Professor of Innovation Studies
The University of Queensland
St Lucia, Australia

David Gann
Professor of Innovation and
Technology Management
Imperial College London
Chair of the UK Atomic Energy Authority
London, UK

CONTENTS

LIST OF FIGURES

CHAPTER 1

What Is Philanthropy and Why Is It Important and Controversial?

Abstract This chapter defines philanthropy and explains why it is so important and controversial. It explains its connections with innovation and entrepreneurship. Philanthropy is defined by its function, form and source. A brief history of philanthropy is provided, including in the USA, UK, China and Germany. The extent of philanthropic giving is described.

Keywords Importance of philanthropy · Controversies in philanthropy · Defining philanthropy · History of philanthropy · Extent of philanthropy

INTRODUCTION

Defined most simply as love of mankind, philanthropy is more practically understood as generous benefaction towards the well-being and happiness of others. Such benevolent giving has had, and continues to have, a profound impact on millions of people, in their health and spirit, in the education they receive, the natural environment they live in and in the civic and political conversations that help determine their future.

Scientific progress and a thriving arts scene depend crucially upon the support of philanthropy. Hospitals, universities, libraries, art galleries, museums and places of worship commonly rely on philanthropic giving.

© The Author(s) 2020
M. Dodgson and D. Gann, *Philanthropy,*
Innovation and Entrepreneurship,
https://doi.org/10.1007/978-3-030-38017-5_1

Philanthropy helps protect the environment by supporting nature conservation and funding thousands of parks and botanical gardens. In both poor and rich nations, philanthropy delivers extensive and wide-ranging benefits, from the provision of clean water and vaccination programmes in Africa to the creation of public service broadcasting and the 911 emergency call service in the USA. Philanthropy has valuably contributed to the fight against the evils of slavery, racial segregation in schools, and denial of educational opportunities for girls.

Yet, despite all the benefits it has conferred, philanthropy remains controversial in, for example, its relationship with the government, and the extent of the way the state can cede the provision of public goods to a few wealthy people. Philanthropy can accentuate and exaggerate political divisions in society. It promotes the liberal agendas of marriage equality and access to birth control and at the same time supports socially conservative causes such as restrictions on the availability of contraception and abortion. This can be argued to further democracy, but it can also powerfully amplify the voices of social discord.

Some of the controversies surrounding philanthropy were illustrated when in September 2018, Jeff Bezos of Amazon announced the gift of $2 billion to help the homeless and establish a new network of schools. Amongst all the positive commentary on this extraordinary benefaction were criticisms that it was not generous enough. Bezos was reputed at the time to be worth more than $160 billion. Questions were raised about the means by which his wealth was accumulated, including exploitative work practices in Amazon distribution centres and the company's expertise at avoiding taxation, and whether, indeed, such gifts are designed to deflect such reproaches. The sensitivities philanthropy arouses are evident when someone can donate $2 billion to good causes and still attract criticism.

The Sackler family has donated hundreds of millions of dollars to some of the highest profile cultural and educational institutions in the world, including the Guggenheim, Smithsonian, Victoria and Albert and British Museums, and Harvard, Oxford and Cambridge Universities. Yet in recent years institutions that have received donations have either refused to accept more funding from the Sackler Trust or removed the Sackler name from the galleries and buildings the Trust has supported. The reason is the Sackler family owns Purdue Pharma, the company accused of promoting opioids: more than 130 people die each day in the USA after overdosing on opioids. The controversy surrounding the Sackler family led to the Sackler Trust announcing in 2019 it was halting all new philanthropic giving. Philanthropists may be making important contributions to good causes, but there is a need to properly assess the sources of their wealth: should "good" be funded by questionable sources?

Another controversy surrounds the concept of "philanthrocapitalism" (Bishop and Green 2008; Edwards 2008), the idea that business principles can be successfully combined with the search for social progress. Proponents contend that the techniques that business people use to accumulate wealth, especially recently in the technology and finance sectors, can be applied to improve the effectiveness and efficiency of philanthropy. Opponents point to a lack of evidence that this is the case, question the accountability of such philanthropists, and ask whether these business methods are indeed superior to socially determined, democratic processes for decision-making. They query whether philanthropic giving is best guided by the business principles of markets and competition or civil society's principles of social justice.

Philanthropy includes donations from wealthy individuals and corporations, often directed through foundations, and it is these that are often most contentious. In his book on American philanthropy, Waldemar Nielson (2002) captures the wide differences of opinions on philanthropy, and especially in philanthropic foundations, saying they can be "inspiring in some the highest hopes and expectations and in others dark fears and resentments. By some they are seen as the Hope of the Future... by others as our Fifth Column".[1]

This Introduction will address the many and varied contributions of philanthropy and its virtues and drawbacks, and analyses the close connections between *philanthropy, innovation*, defined as the successful application of new ideas, and *entrepreneurship*, defined by opportunity recognition and risk-taking. It will analyse when philanthropy is society's hope of the future and when a fifth column. It offers a multidisciplinary and international perspective, and includes case studies and vignettes of leading philanthropists and philanthropic organizations, past and present. It considers the future challenges of philanthropy and how it can best support innovation and innovation can support it. It develops the argument that the greatest contribution philanthropy can make is when it supports innovation and entrepreneurship that improves human welfare and well-being and would not occur in its absence.

DEFINING PHILANTHROPY

Philanthropy is a very diverse phenomenon, and distinguishing it from other forms of giving is notoriously difficult. Definitions of philanthropy are often conflated with related activities such as charity; social enterprises, entrepreneurship and innovation; non-profit and non-governmental organizations; the voluntary and "third" sector, and "impact investing" (investing to produce positive social and environmental, as well as financial, returns). There is confusion because there is overlap in all these various activities and organizations, and philanthropy can support them all. They often provide the means by which philanthropy is delivered. But they are different, and confusion often reigns.

The bewildering range of organizations, structures and activities described as philanthropy does not help research and analysis to build cumulative understanding. Legal definitions of philanthropy tend to very broad and, in any case, vary across national jurisdictions, making internationally comparative analysis very challenging. Yet, greater clarity is needed, and a clear definition of philanthropy is required.

The Oxford English Dictionary offers the following definition:

> *Love of mankind; the disposition or active effort to promote the happiness and well-being of others; practical benevolence, now esp. as expressed by the generous donation of money to good causes.*

But is giving to a good cause by buying a badge from a street fundraiser or running a sponsored marathon the same as a systematic campaign of substantial and engaged support for promoting the happiness and well-being of others?

Any definitions will be tendentious, and there will be exceptions to any rule. Nevertheless, for analysis to be meaningful some categorization and boundaries of philanthropy have to be determined, and we shall concentrate particularly on what can be considered "strategic" philanthropy. This form of philanthropy can be distinguished by its function, form and source.

The *function* of this philanthropic giving is active involvement with enacting lasting change. One way of distinguishing philanthropy and charity, for example, is associating the former with addressing the causes of problems and the latter with the effects of those problems. Words commonly used to describe charity often include palliative, rescue and relief, and philanthropy include corrective, rebuilding and problem-solving. Yet many charities address causes of problems, such as cancer research, and engage in policy work designed to correct social problems. Using a retailing analogy, charity has been likened to high-street retailing with many stores and products from which to choose, and philanthropy with expensive bespoke purchasing. One benefactor has said that when he simply writes a cheque it is charity, but when he dedicates his time, energy and money towards a cause he passionately believes in, it is philanthropy. In such a view, philanthropy is active, and charity is passive. But again, this is not always the case.

In this book, the position is taken that the function of philanthropy lies with its providers' wish to determine how the problems with which they have strongly emotionally identified are to be tackled. Philanthropy, in the words of John D. Rockefeller (1909), deals with "finalities – a search for a cause, an attempt to cure evils at their source". In 1904, Joseph Rowntree wrote a Founder's Memorandum for his Foundation in which he says:

> I feel that much of the current philanthropic effort is directed to remedying the more superficial manifestations of weakness or evil, while little thought or effort is directed to search out their underlying causes. Obvious distress or evil generally evokes so much feeling that the necessary agencies for alleviating it are pretty adequately supported. For example, it is much easier to obtain funds for the famine-stricken people in India than to originate and carry through a searching enquiry into the causes and recurrence of these famines.[2]

In the words of the great British entrepreneur and philanthropist, Dame Steve (Stephanie) Shirley: "charity repairs the immediate damage of social ills, philanthropy tries in a more preventative way to make society a better place. For those who can afford to give large sums, philanthropy is a more productive investment" (Shirley 2012).

In the delivery of its aims and objectives it is clearly not the function of philanthropy to make profits.

The *form* that philanthropy takes is usually manifested in a formal, professional organization. These are commonly foundations that have charitable status. Many charities are similar in form to foundations, but a substantial number of them are much more informal and unstructured. In the

UK, there may be more unregistered charities—usually very small organizations—than those registered with the regulator, the Charities Commission.[3] Many companies operate foundations to manage their philanthropic giving. While philanthropic foundations fund charities, they also fund other activities such as social entrepreneurship as means to further social progress. Philanthropic giving, in intent at least, most commonly occurs through knowledgeable and proficient foundations or other formal organizations that have clearly established processes that solicit or respond to proposals for funding that can take the form of grants, gifts or contracts.

The most studied *source* of strategic philanthropic giving tends to be wealthy (high net worth) people, and corporations, donating significant amounts. These donations are directed often but not exclusively to foundations and charities, such as those delivering aid, or supporting universities or Arts organizations. In combination, the contributions of smaller amounts from a larger population of people are more significant than giving from wealthy people and corporations. The capacity of these resources to deliver on the functions of philanthropy depends upon how they are marshalled and managed, and this may take the form of foundations and charities. Philanthropy usually involves the donation of money, time and expertise, but also includes amongst its sources an emotional attachment to the objective of their giving.

The approach taken here is concerned with the most common and usual practices, an *ideal type*, attempting to capture generalities while appreciating that there are specific variations and occasional blurred boundaries. Generally, however, philanthropy can be considered as giving that directly attempt to *affect* opportunities for social progress by influencing the causes of the problems and issues of concern to donors.

Using this definition helps to circumscribe a very disparate phenomenon, which assists with analysis, but appreciates at the same time it reduces its richness and the diversity in the way people give, in different ways and across different cultures. In this way, this book on philanthropy is about a specific, important and powerful form of benefaction, but it recognizes the significance of, and connections with, other ways of giving.

SOME CONTROVERSIES

Despite the enormous resources devoted to philanthropy, and the many important contributions it has made, the diversity of opinion about philanthropy is profound and of considerable contemporary significance all around in the world. In the USA, for example, advocates, such as Karl Zinsmeister (2006), from the Philanthropy Roundtable, says philanthropy "is a huge part of what makes America America", especially in the celebration of personal freedom, and the economist Zoltan Acs (2013) claims "it has been an essential ingredient of American capitalism". Those with a more critical perspective, such as author David Callahan (2017), caution about the way philanthropy allows rich people to apply their ideologies and religious beliefs to influence crucial social and economic issues. He says philanthropic foundations "are incomparable vehicles for amplifying the influence that wealthy private citizens can have over society". Theda Skocpol (2016) cautions that: "giving so much authority over vital civic resources to wealthy donors undermines democratic governance in many ways", and continues that: "On issues such as taxes, climate change, health reform, and the role of government generally, politically active, wealthy philanthropists are fueling partisan polarization and, in key instances, influencing policy agendas toward the ultra-free-market right". For Robert Reich (2019) philanthropy is often an exercise of power, the conversion of private assets into public influence that is largely unaccountable and lavishly tax-advantaged. Linsey McGoey (2015), through her criticisms of the Gates Foundation, and other philanthropic organizations established by technology entrepreneurs, questions the self-interest of donors. Anand Giridharadas (2018) questions the motives of many wealthy people, and points to their frequent desire for public recognition.

These critical views reflect the earlier strident criticisms of Italian Marxist Antonio Gramsci who saw philanthropy as a means by which capitalists maintained their hegemonic control of the market and workers, and averted attention away from the concentration of wealth in the hands of few people (Gramsci 1917).

It is in America where this debate is particularly pressing, because philanthropy is a significantly larger phenomenon there than elsewhere in the world. In some nations with strong civic societies, such as in Scandinavia, philanthropy is less important and can even be denigrated as the privilege of plutocrats and paternalists. Yet philanthropy is becoming an ever more central issue as governments everywhere struggle to fund demands beyond the willingness of tax payers to pay for them, and corporations become ever more short-term in their perspectives. There is no shortage of problems in society to be addressed: poverty, ignorance, inequality in opportunity, ill-health and environmental degradation, that require solutions that are innovative and imaginative, concerted and well-funded. According to UNICEF, about 29,000 children under the age of five die every day, mainly from preventable causes. There is a growing recognition right throughout the world that philanthropy can play a crucial and positive role in addressing these challenges. As a result, there needs to be an informed debate about the phenomenon and practice of philanthropy, the government policies that support it, and the innovation it can provide.

A Brief History

The USA is presently the largest provider of philanthropic giving, and many observers argue its intimate association with the evolution of American capitalism and the ardent historical promotion of individual freedom as opposed to what are seen as the incursions of the government. According to Acs (2013), the cycle of giving—from philanthropy to new opportunity creation—has been an essential ingredient of American capitalism throughout the country's history. He says Americans' motivations for giving money, as well as the outputs of their generosity, are woven into the entrepreneurial spirit of the nation. The historian Olivier Zunz (2011) chronicles the tight connections between private giving and public affairs in the USA, and argues this union has enlarged its democracy and shaped its history. Giving for the betterment of all, he contends, has become embedded in the fabric of the nation's civic democracy.

Acs suggests philanthropy is an American invention, and it has welcomed entrepreneurial activity and encouraged vast amounts of wealth creation, but it has tended to avoid the establishment of a ruling class. This he contrasts with Europe in modern history where "the wealthy had money because they were from the nobility and they were the nobility because they were wealthy". In an entrepreneurial society such as America, by contrast, he contends people are wealthy because they have worked hard and seized opportunity. American philanthropy he suggests uses money to create systems of opportunity and innovation in their own society. In Western Europe, where there is far less philanthropy, he claims the capitalist system is supported almost entirely by the state, claiming it is difficult to find examples where European philanthropy has actually strengthened institutions of capitalism in Europe.

This view rather ignores the lengthy history of philanthropy in other countries and the wide diversity in relationships between philanthropy and governments around the world. Historian Frank Prochaska (1990) says no country on earth can lay claim to a greater philanthropic tradition than Great Britain, and many nations, such as China, have supported benevolent giving since antiquity. Previously almost the exclusive privilege of the aristocracy and landed gentry, the industrial revolution in Britain produced new sources of wealth and rich individuals concerned with supporting good causes. The early industrialist Josiah Wedgwood financially supported artists, including Joshua Reynolds and George Stubbs. Wedgwood made and freely distributed scientific instruments to scientists such as Lavoisier and Priestley and backed the latter's experiments. His wealth allowed his sons to help establish the Royal Horticultural Society and assist in the development of photography, and it underpinned the scientific career of his grandson, Charles Darwin (Dodgson 2011). The advance of entrepreneurs and industry produced the wealth to support the progress of science and the arts.

The role of benevolent organizations was integral to Victorian Britain. Dr. Barnardo's (1867) and the National Society for the Prevention of Cruelty to Children (1884), for example, addressed the immense disadvantages of children. Prochaska (1990) provides evidence that in the eighteenth and nineteenth centuries families at all levels of the society gave tithes—a tenth of their income—to worthy causes, and suggests some individuals at the time gave away millions of pounds. He refers to a study of middle-class households in the 1890s that established that on average they spent a larger share of their income on good causes than on any item in their budget except food. Philanthropy certainly had a profound impact on British society. William Wilberforce explained the campaign against slavery was grounded on the principles of philanthropy. By encouraging Victorian women to engage with social causes, and demonstrate the value and rewards of this labour, philanthropy contributed to the emancipation of women.

There has been a long tradition of generous giving in Asia (Jang 2018). The roots of Chinese philanthropy, for example, go back many centuries, with giving deeply embedded in Confucian, Buddhist and Daoist ethics. In describing the history of philanthropy in China, Chen et al. (2014)

argue how: "Motivated by a mix of religious inclination, moral obligation, and loyalty to native place, individuals sponsored the building of temples, schools, orphanages, and hospitals; provided relief during famine and in the aftermath of natural disasters". These authors show how social organizations provided assistance to the needy before the Qin dynasty (211BCE). During the Tang dynasty (618–907), government sponsored Buddhist temples to establish soup kitchens and medical dispensaries to serve the poor. During the Song dynasty (960–1279) until the end of imperial rule in 1912, poorhouses and orphanages were sponsored by magistrates and "charitable estates" held and operated by family lineages. Benevolent societies, privately founded and funded, emerged in the Ming dynasty (1368–1644) helping distribute food and bury the poor. In the Qing dynasty (1644–1912), there was an increase in private benefaction mainly focussed on places of birth. During the nineteenth century local philanthropy was joined by foreign giving, especially by missionaries and with a focus on establishing hospitals. During the 1920s the French Pasteur Institute, for example, gave to church-sponsored hospitals, donating eight new American X-ray machines.

The Rockefeller Foundation has played a crucial role in the development of modern medicine in China (Schneider 2002). The China Medical Board was founded in 1914 to bring recent medical science to China, and it received two tranches of funding from the Rockefellers, in 1928 and 1947. Initially, a division of the Rockefeller Foundation the Board became independent after the 1947 investment. Rockefeller has also played substantial roles in supporting universities, public health and rural reconstruction in China.

Foreign philanthropy was barred during the Mao era. The Ford Foundation, however, played a significant role in encouraging academic research and international understanding about China during this period. The Ford Foundation only began to operate in the country in 1978, and currently has significant programmes in the environment, culture, poverty alleviation and education in remote areas.

It is difficult to assess the extent of philanthropy in China, but it is clear a rapid expansion is occurring, seen for example in the activities of the increasing group of the super wealthy prepared to invest in philanthropic causes. At the same time, the State has withdrawn from the position that it was solely responsible for the total provision of social welfare services, allowing space for the introduction of philanthropic giving. The State retains its central role, however, with significant regulation of, particularly overseas, philanthropic activities.

Even Germany, which after the reforms introduced by Bismarck is often held to be strongly statist, has a long tradition of influential philanthropy. Thomas Adam (2016) argues in the nineteenth century: "public institutions such as museums, high schools, universities, hospitals, and social-housing enterprises were unable to survive without the support of wealthy donors. State funding for universities and high schools, for instance, accounted only for a fragment of the operating costs of these institutions". The Carl-Zeiss-Stiftung,[4] for example, was established by Ernst Abbe in 1889 to advance science and education at the University of Jena. Private funds were also invested in other German research institutes, for instance a multitude of private investors created the Institute for Cancer Research in Heidelberg in 1903.

The development of the Zeppelin relied on private giving: the German military establishment and Kaiser Wilhelm II were sceptical about the value of airships, but after a 1908 drive for funding from the public, further development of the product by Count Ferdinand von Zeppelin revealed its potential.

German families were influential. The philanthropy of Ludwig Mond and his two sons Alfred and Robert is told by Adam (2016), and includes support for: "art collecting, the fight against early childhood mortality, the advancement of research and of higher education, archaeological excavations in Egypt and Palestine, and for the founding of the State of Israel from the 1890s to the late 1930s. These activities resulted in the creation of the Bibliotheca Hertziana in Rome, the donation of Ludwig Mond's art collection to the National Gallery in London, the funding of the excavation of the sacred Buchis Bulls at Armant in Egypt, the establishment of the Children's Hospital in London, and the support of many natural science institutes and associations in England, France, Germany, and Italy".

In many countries, the relationship between philanthropy and government has changed and evolved over time. The role of philanthropy in Britain changed with the post-second world war growth of the welfare state, and in the Mao era in China the contribution of philanthropy was dismissed as every aspect of life was controlled by the authority of government. America has never assumed such a role for the government, and philanthropy has played a continuingly important role in the

provision of social goods and in the political economy. Alexis De Tocqueville, the Frenchman visiting the USA in the 1830s to study its prison
system, argued that the success of the new country heavily depended
on giving and voluntary associations. He concludes: "In the United
States associations are established to promote public order, commerce,
industry, morality, and religion; for there is no end which the human will,
seconded by the collective exertions of individuals, despairs of attaining"
(De Tocqueville 1835). Engrained politically, economically and socially
in the USA, it is also a powerful element of the way many understand
a central element of the nation's zeitgeist. Zinsmeister (2006), from the
Philanthropy Roundtable—which describes itself as "America's leading
network of charitable donors working to strengthen our free society,
uphold donor intent, and protect the freedom to give" emphasizes this
centrality. He says America's social order is devoted to freedom and
goodness, that philanthropy allows a good society without a paternalistic
state, and it is the guardian of self-rule. There is no doubting the "hope
of the future" view of philanthropy in some circles.

Nor is there doubt of the extent of giving, with total donations in
the USA in 2015 exceeding $373 billion. America has over 1.5 million
tax-exempt organizations, including 900,000 public charities, 100,000
private foundations and around 320,000 religious congregations. Zinsmeister (2006) suggests 14% of charitable funding in the USA comes
from foundations and 5% from corporations, the rest comes from individuals giving an annual $2500 a household. Given the definition of
philanthropy we have adopted our primary interest lies with giving by
foundations and corporations, which accounts for about $75 billion in
donations in 2015. These categories of giving are likely to increase in
significance. Callahan (2017) reports some 30,000 new private foundations were created in the 15 years to 2015, along with 185,000 so-called
donor-advised funds, which provide a structured and tax-efficient method
of giving. He states that in the 10 years from 2005 over 14,000 gifts of
$1 million or more were made to colleges and universities, and at least
100 of these were worth over $100 million. Health institutions attracted
nearly 5000 gifts of $1 million or more, with at least two topping a
half-billion dollars. Arts and cultural institutions received 4000 gifts of
$1 million and up each during this same period.

The extent of philanthropy in the UK is smaller in scale than the
USA's, but is increasing in significance. Total giving in 2016 was £17.8
billion, around 0.2% of government spending, however it is argued, for

reasons to be expanded upon later, to be disproportionately influential. Foundation giving is highly skewed, with the Wellcome Trust in 2016 giving away more than the next 17 largest UK foundations combined. The top 300 charitable foundations in the UK are responsible for 90% of foundation giving.

The ten-year anniversary of the Coutts Million Pound Donors Report found that nearly £15 billion in million pound plus gifts has been given in total by individuals, foundations or corporations in the decade to 2017. The total value of donations of £1 million or more rose from £1.37 billion in 2006/07 to a record high of £1.83 billion in 2016. Foundations were the largest source of donations of £1 million or more over the 10-year period, totalling 64% of the total number (1558) and over half of the total value (£7.67 billion). The total value of corporate donations rose from just under £50 million in 2006/07 to over £500 million in 2016. The Report shows the most common amount given is exactly £1 million (Coutts 2017).

The contribution of some philanthropists can be remarkable, seen, for example, in the following list of buildings supported by the Sainsbury family in the UK, noting that the Sainsbury family trusts provide many other forms of support. The buildings house science and medicine, the arts in various forms and social science.

Sainsbury family contributions to public and research buildings
Sainsbury Centre for Visual Arts, University of East Anglia
Sainsbury Laboratory, Norwich
Sainsbury Laboratory, University of Cambridge
Sainsbury Wing, National Gallery, London
Sainsbury Library, University of Oxford
Sainsbury African Galleries, and Exhibitions Gallery, British Museum, London
Timothy Sainsbury Gallery, Victoria and Albert Museum, London
Robert and Lisa Sainsbury Wing, Hammersmith Hospital, London
Sainsbury-Wellcome Centre for Neural Circuits and Behaviour, University College London.
Linbury Gallery, Tate Britain, London
Linbury Gallery, Museum of London
Linbury Gallery, Royal Welsh College of Music & Drama, Cardiff
Linbury Studio Theatre, Royal Opera House, London
Linbury Studio, London Academy of Music and Dramatic Art

Headley Lecture Theatre in the Ashmolean Museum, University of Oxford
Raven Row Art Gallery, London
Centre for Mental Health, London
National STEM Learning Centre, University of York
Centre for Justice Innovation, London
Astor Community Theatre, Deal, Kent

Having described some of the controversies surrounding philanthropy, and established its scope and scale and something of its history, we now turn to asking who are philanthropists and why do they give?

NOTES

1. A *fifth column* is a clandestine group of people who undermine a larger group from within.
2. https://www.jrf.org.uk/about-us/our-heritage/lasting-vision-change.
3. https://www.gov.uk/government/organisations/charity-commission.
4. A Stiftung is a not for profit foundation. The Carl-Zeiss-Stiftung is the foundation that is the overarching owner of two significant companies: Carl Zeiss AG and Schott AG.

REFERENCES

Acs, Z. (2013). *Why Philanthropy Matters*. Princeton, NJ: Princeton University Press.

Adam, T. (2016). *Transnational Philanthropy: The Mond Family's Support for Public Institutions in Western Europe from 1890 to 1938*. Palgrave Macmillan.

Bishop, M., & Green, M. (2008). *Philanthrocapitalism: How the Rich Can Save the World*. New York, NY: Bloomsbury Press.

Callahan, D. (2017). *The Givers: Wealth, Power, and Philanthropy in a New Gilded Age*. New York: Knopf.

Chen, L., Ryan, J., & Saich, A. (2014). Introduction: Philanthropy for Health in China: Distinctive Roots and Future Prospects. In J. Ryan, L. C. Chen, & A. J. Saich (Eds.), *Philanthropy for Health in China*. Bloomington: Indiana University Press.

Coutts Million Pound Donors Report. (2017). *Coutts Million Pound Donors Report 2017*. London: Coutts. https://www.coutts.com/insight-articles/news/2017/million-pound-donors-report-2017.html.

De Tocqueville, A. (1835 [2000]). *Democracy in America*. Chicago: University of Chicago Press.

Dodgson, M. (2011). Exploring New Combinations in Innovation and Entrepreneurship: Social Networks, Schumpeter, and the Case of Josiah Wedgwood (1730–1795). *Industrial and Corporate Change, 20*(4), 1119–1151.

Edwards, M. (2008). *Just Another Emperor? The Myths and Realities of Philanthrocapitalism*. Demos: The Young Foundation.

Giridharadas, A. (2018). *Winners Take All: The Elite Charade of Changing the World*. New York: Penguin Random House.

Gramsci, A. (1917, December 24). Philanthropy, Good Will and Organization. *Avanti!*

Jang, H. (2018). Old Money—The History of Giving in Asia. In R. Shapiro, M. Mirchandani, & H. Jang (Eds.), *Pragmatic Philanthropy: Asian Charity Explained*. Singapore: Palgrave Macmillan.

McGoey, L. (2015). *No Such Thing as a Free Gift*. London: Verso.

Nielson, W. (2002). *Golden Donors*. New Brunswick, NJ: Transaction Publishers.

Prochaska, F. (1990). Philanthropy. In F. Thompson (Ed.), *The Cambridge Social History of Britain* (pp. 1750–1950). Cambridge: Cambridge University Press.

Reich, R. (2019). *Just Giving: Why Philanthropy Is Failing Democracy and How It Can Do Better*. Princeton, NJ: Princeton University Press.

Rockefeller, J. (1909 [2013]). *Random Reminiscences of Man and Events*. New York: Creative English Publishers.

Schneider, W. (2002). *Rockefeller Philanthropy and Modern Biomedicine: International Initiatives from World War I to the Cold War*. Bloomington, IN: Indiana University Press.

Shirley, S. (2012). *Let IT Go*. Andrews, UK.

Skocpol, T. (2016). Politics Symposium: Why Political Scientists Should Study Organized Philanthropy. *PS Political Science and Politics, 49*(3), 433–436.

Zinsmeister, K. (2006). How Philanthropy Fuels American Success. In *The Almanac of American Philanthropy*. Washington, DC: Philanthropy Roundtable.

Zunz, O. (2011). *Philanthropy in America: A History*. Princeton: Princeton University Press.

CHAPTER 2

Who Are Philanthropists and Why Do They Give?

Abstract This chapter explores the motivations and personalities of philanthropists, analysing the question of why they give. Numerous examples of wealthy donors are discussed. A novel analysis of the Giving Pledge is provided. The importance of religion is considered. The debate over the importance of tax incentives for encouraging philanthropy is outlined.

Keywords Motivations of philanthropists · Examples of philanthropists · Analysis of Giving Pledge · Philanthropy and religion · Philanthropy and tax

Wealthy Benefactors

The benefactions of some philanthropists are astronomical in scale. When in 2006, Warren Buffett began to gradually give away 85% of his shares in his company, they were valued at $37 billion. In 2015, Mark Zuckerberg and Priscilla Chan pledged to donate 99% of their Facebook shares valued at $45 billion at the time to the Chan Zuckerberg Initiative.

The wealth that philanthropists accumulate is often derived from innovation and entrepreneurship, and this is especially the case with recent generations of technology and financial entrepreneurs. Many philanthropists use the approaches they developed in creating their wealth

© The Author(s) 2020   17
M. Dodgson and D. Gann, *Philanthropy, Innovation and Entrepreneurship*,
https://Doi.org/10.1007/978-3-030-38017-5_2

to subsequently distribute it, and understanding their purpose and modus operandi reveals much about contemporary philanthropy (see e.g. Schervish 2003). The definition of entrepreneur used is someone who sees an opportunity and is prepared to take risks, and this captures much of the nature and behaviours of philanthropists (see e.g. Dodgson and Gann 2018).

Philanthropists differ in character as much as the general population. Although many are larger-than-life, and their deeds can be extraordinarily generous and devoted to the most publicly minded of causes, some philanthropists have accumulated their wealth through nefarious means and they are not always the most likeable of people.

Leland Stanford, the eponymous founder of Stanford University, shamelessly used his position in the US Senate to further his interests in railroads through disreputable methods. John Rockefeller Snr. built Standard Oil by highly questionable monopolistic business practices. At an industrial dispute at a company he controlled, in a day-long fight with strikers the Colorado National Guard killed around two dozen, including two women and 11 children asphyxiated in a burning tent. The Ludlow Massacre as it was known was an especially notorious element of a dispute with miners that eventually killed up to 200 people. Andrew Carnegie came to regret the brutal breaking of an 1892 strike by his workers which cost ten lives. He might also be dismayed at the way his Foundation-funded research into eugenics that was valued by the Nazis.

Giving away vast amounts of wealth does not necessarily imply philanthropists have warm and sociable personalities. Some, such as Howard Hughes, are notoriously strange, and some are fiercely competitive. John Olin, of Olin Industries and the Olin Foundation, said "show me a good loser and I'll show you a loser". And some are especially miserly in their day-to-day behaviours. Sebastian Kresge, founder of K-Mart, a man who gave $60 million away, is reputed to have given up golf because he couldn't abide the cost of lost golf balls.

George Eastman, founder of Kodak, funded the early development of MIT and created the Eastman School of Music at the University of Rochester. His extensive philanthropy included being the biggest contributor to African-American education in the 1920s. Eastman insisted his company use a calendar of 13 months each of 28 days. He awoke and breakfasted each morning to the sounds of a live musician on the organ he had installed in his house. Inquiring of his doctor one day the exact location of his heart he returned home, placed a gun to it and shot himself dead.

Amongst his other benefactions, John Paul Getty, the wealthy oil-man, endowed the Getty Center in Los Angeles with one of the world's greatest art collections, generously ensuring that entry would always be free. Married and divorced five times, Getty combined the most refined tastes—he spoke numerous languages and was an expert art collector—with an innate personal meanness. When his grandson was kidnapped he at first refused to pay the ransom. After his grandson's severed ear was sent through the post as a warning of worse to come he relented and offered $2 million, the maximum allowed as a tax deduction, and lent his son the remainder of the demand at 4% interest.

Personal eccentricities apart, many philanthropists and foundations are dedicated to promoting progressive causes. The Buffett Foundation is a major supporter of women's access to low-cost contraception and rights to abortion. Howard Buffett is promoting sustainable agriculture and building hydro-electricity plants in Africa, often working in some of the most dangerous countries in the world. George Soros has supported causes such as same-sex marriage, softening drugs laws, and Black Lives Matters. Michael Bloomberg gives, amongst other causes, to the Arts, stopping smoking, reducing traffic deaths in developing countries, dealing with climate change, gun control and better managing fish stocks. Climate change is a concern of many philanthropists, with benefactors such as Tom Steyer and his NextGen Climate initiative and the Pritzker Innovation Fund, which works mainly on climate and energy issues, attempting to influence the political debate. The work of some foundations can be surprising in their progressive agendas given the reactionary politics of some of their founders. In the 1960s, the Ford Foundation—founded by the extremely right-wing Henry Ford—supported civil rights through education, voter registration drives and community action programmes, and by funding substantial research programmes to support mutual understanding eased tension in the China/America relationship during the Mao era.

More men than women are remembered for their philanthropy, although many women have made significant contributions. Donations from women to higher education institutions in the nineteenth century commonly stipulated that their giving was conditional on the admission of females, and often required the provision of new career opportunities for women. Many women have been leaders in faith-based philanthropy.

Women played a core role in Quaker philanthropy, for example, which since the seventeenth century has assisted fellow members who had fallen on hard times (Freeman 2013). The appalling conditions for the poor in nineteenth-century London were addressed by social reformers such as Emma Cons and Lucy Cavendish (Geddes Poole 2014). By organizing women's philanthropic campaigns, women asserted their civic role.

Born in London and raised in poverty in the mid-West prairie, Ellen Browning Scripps, along with her brother, built America's largest chain of newspapers. Worth around $30 million in 1920, she gave most of it away to her favoured causes of women's education, the labour movement and public access to science, the arts and education. Amongst other enduring institutions she funded Scripps Institution of Oceanography in La Jolla, California and Scripps College in Claremont, California (McClain 2017). Katharine McCormick, heir to the International Harvester fortune, was the sole funder of Gregory Pincus's development of contraceptive pill. She insisted on going to collect her own prescription of the pill aged into her 80s.

Women have also played a crucial role in encouraging and directing philanthropic giving from wealth accumulated by their husbands or fathers. Many foundations are named after husbands and wives, recognizing the contributions both made to the accumulation of wealth and the decisions leading to its dispersal. Of the 171 signatories to the Giving Pledge (see below) in 2018, 91 were from couples, 68 from men and 12 from women. Nowadays more women are becoming influential philanthropists by donating wealth of their own making, and many of these women, such as Sheryl Sandberg, built their careers in the technology industry. Anounsheh Ansari, an engineer, financed a prize for the first private craft to transport three people into space, and her intervention has stimulated much greater investment in the industry. By any measure, Melinda Gates is one of the most important, committed and skilled philanthropists of all time.

Many celebrities support philanthropic organizations (see e.g. Jeffreys and Allatson 2015). Some are associated with particular causes, such as Oprah Winfrey and schooling for African girls and Elton John for his foundation's work on AIDS. Others are linked with disabilities or diseases from which they have suffered, such as Christopher Reeve and work on paralysis and Michael J. Fox on Parkinson's disease. Groups of celebrities contribute to causes such as Live Aid, Comic Relief and Make Poverty History. U2's Bono was featured alongside Bill and Melinda Gates on the cover of *Time* magazine as 2005's people of the year for their work on addressing poverty. Associating celebrities with causes can valuably raise awareness and attract additional funding, but can also induce ridicule if there is too much contrast between the causes they support and the excessive lifestyles they enjoy.

WHY DO THEY GIVE?

In 1749, Henry Fielding in *Tom Jones* wrote that in philanthropy "there is a great and exquisite Delight". History is full of examples of individuals who have taken great delight in dispensing their wealth. As one of Britain's most generous philanthropists, Dame Steve (Stephanie) Shirley (2012), put it, giving her money away has given her considerably more rewards than earning it in the first place. In her book, *Let It Go*, Steve Shirley writes a deeply personal account of her extraordinary life's journey. As a very early software entrepreneur she became extremely wealthy. Did she value that wealth, she asked herself? "Yes, it was nice to think that I would never again have to worry myself sick about how I was going to pay the bills... If you had ever been poor, as I had, you tend to vow, as soon as you are in a position to do so, that you will never be poor again". But she recognized there's a limit to the number of fine dinners you can have, and she has no enthusiasm for yachts, jets and multiple homes. Her pleasure lay instead in realizing the opportunities of using her wealth to do good. She has supported a variety of causes, all close to her heart and interests, especially in supporting research into autism, and says that her giving has made her feel truly fortunate: Giving may be a duty, she has written, but it is above all a pleasure.

Acs (2013) says philanthropy is woven into the cultural fabric of America and into the entrepreneurial middle-class values that founded the country and sustained its prosperity. But the bottom line is that philanthropists do not have to give their money away. There is no law instructing them to do so. As Peter Singer (2015), the Princeton University moral philosopher, puts it: giving away large sums is not a sensible strategy for increasing personal wealth. There may be tax advantages, and compelling social, cultural and religious incentives, but in the end, it comes down to the individual's decision about what to do with their wealth, and this often reflects their values, interests and concerns. While some give for reasons of self-promotion or advance, others undoubtedly are, as Abraham Lincoln put it, touched by the better angels of our nature. Some feel a sense of responsibility, of *noblesse oblige*. Individuals can be extraordinarily generous. For many this reflects a human concern for others and belief, often handed down through generations, that people have a duty to help the less fortunate. As it is put in the King James Bible: "For unto whomsoever much is given, of him shall be much required". A key ethical question, according to Peter Singer, is how much they should give. The rich, he says, should give. But what, he asks, is the moral equivalence of someone giving away 5 or 35% of their wealth?

One distinction is between those who give for pure altruistic reasons, a selfless willingness to help others, and those whose giving back is motivated by an acknowledgment (or guilt) that one has received more than their fair share in life, even through their own merits, and want to share with or give some of this surplus back to society.

Many find giving to be personally rewarding. Julius Rosenwald, one of America's greatest philanthropists who funded the building of nearly 5000 schools educating African Americans in Southern States, said there is no enduring superiority save that which comes as a result of serving (Perkins 2011). Bill Gates says that those who do not give their money away miss out on the opportunity to make an impact, learn a lot and be fulfilled. Warren Buffet has called the act of giving a "joyous mission". Philanthropist James Chen puts it eloquently when he says his experience in setting up and leading the development of his Foundation opened up a new world of opportunity, leading him on a deeply meaningful life journey; one that he found both challenging and fulfilling.

Some give because of personal circumstances. Milton Hershey, founder of the chocolate bar empire, who could have no children himself, gave his entire fortune away to house and educate orphans. Leland Stanford and his wife, Jane, gave their fortune away to memorialize their only child who died of typhoid fever. John D. Rockefeller's grandson died from Scarlet Fever, stimulating his interest in medical research. Sergei Brin, from Google, supports research into Parkinson's disease, which his mother has. David Koch from Koch Industries and investor Michael Milliken funded research into prostate cancer from which they suffered. Eli Broad supports research into Crohn's disease, which struck his son. Olivia Sage was proud of her descent from her ancestor, Miles Standish, who arrived in America on the Mayflower. After naming a Hall at Harvard after Standish, she was delighted to say how her ancestors would tell her "well done", and how "they could well hold up their heads and be as proud as I am of their works" (Crocker 2005).

Some philanthropists pursue their passions as collectors in order to share and let others benefit from their enthusiasms, passions and idiosyncrasies. Lord Ashcroft, for example, has acquired the largest collection of Victoria Crosses in the world. These medals, which reward the highest levels of military bravery, are on public display at the Ashcroft Gallery in the Imperial War Museum in London. Howard Buffet has established a 6000-acre cheetah reserve in South Africa and supports the International Gorilla Conservation Programme, investing to prevent poaching. Nathan Myhrvold, a former chief technology officer at Microsoft, has invested heavily in discovering fossil remains of Tyrannosaurus Rex, and hedge fund owner Ray Dalio is hunting for an elusive giant squid.

Philanthropic bequeaths can occasionally seem a little eccentric. One of the most prestigious professorships at Cambridge University is the Jacksonian Professorship of Natural Philosophy, founded in 1782 by a gift from the Reverend Richard Jackson. He specified that the professor should come from four English counties, Staffordshire, Warwickshire, Derbyshire and Cheshire, and the recipient should search for a cure for gout.

To understand the phenomenon of philanthropy it is necessary to consider the motivations for giving that are not altruistic. Prochaska's (1990) examination of giving in eighteenth- and nineteenth-century Britain points to the social impacts of philanthropy, such as the way it enabled collective action across class lines. He argues: "Whatever one's station, contributions to philanthropic causes were a sign of that much sought after status, respectability. For those with social ambition, contact with better-off neighbours was essential. It acted as a spring-board for many working people who wished to integrate into the existing social and economic system".

"Philanthropy is the gateway to power" is a line taken from the TV series *Mad Men* about 1950s advertising executives. Prochaska argues that in nineteenth-century Britain the ruling classes largely took it for granted that deference would flow from their philanthropy. Some give in the expectation of future favours or civic awards. Ruth Shapiro (2018) argues that while there is great variation throughout Asia, there is a tendency to give first and foremost to family and clan. Asians commonly donate as a function of personal contacts as well as to organizations that expand their business networks. Thus, donations typically enhance personal and business relationships while also providing support to some beneficial work.

Enhancing influence, and hence power, extends into politics. Philanthropists such as Conrad Hilton and Herbert Hoover passionately opposed communism and used their wealth to fight it. Acs (2013) argues that philanthropy and capitalism are symbiotic, with the strength of one reinforcing the strength of the other and vice versa. And historically, philanthropy has been loyal to the institutions of American capitalism. The history of American philanthropy is replete with examples of donors keen on promoting their understanding of freedom, which often takes the form of unfettered capitalism and hostility to government intervention, especially in the economy and education. Their libertarianism is captured in the words of J. Howard Pew, who wrote in the mandate for the Freedom Trust that he created of "the paralyzing effects of government controls on the lives and activities of people", and the "American priceless heritage of freedom and self-determination", compared to the "false promises of socialism and a planned economy" (Sparks 2016).

The history of philanthropic giving in the USA is not, however, one of relentless victories over a subservient state. The government periodically reconsiders the role of philanthropy in society. The first of these was the congressional 1915 Walsh Commission, which at a time of great public concern over the power of powerful companies and trusts, examined the influence of corporate philanthropy on American politics and society. Amongst those summoned and questioned were Andrew Carnegie, John Rockefeller Senior and Junior, and Henry Ford.

There remain many voices disquieted by the continuing power of some philanthropists. Jane Mayer (2016) provides a sobering account of the impact of the long-term strategy of a small number of very wealthy people on politics in the USA. She accounts for the way Charles and David Koch in particular, but others with similar libertarian if not extreme right-wing views, have systematically, and often surreptitiously, used tax-exempt foundations to support their political positions. She traces the influence of their investments in think tanks, lobbying organizations and universities, and the manner in which they have supported movements such as the Tea Party. She details how they encouraged legislation allowing them to increase investments in their favoured causes and prevented legislation that regulates their businesses in areas such as environmental controls.

Francie Ostrower's (1997) book on the philosophy of the elite was based on interviews with 99 wealthy people in the New York area. She found them very diverse, but with some similar views in common. They shared a belief in individualism and private initiative and a mistrust of the government, and a deep conviction of the beneficial contribution of philanthropy which she argues is connected to their conceptions of how society should be organized. Ostrower found great loyalty and concern for particular causes with which the philanthropists identified. They were highly critical of wealthy people who did not make adequate contributions. Giving to causes, and especially the way this was rewarded by recognitions such as Board memberships of important institutions, was seen as affirmation of class status. She says philanthropy helps legitimize their positions in society, allowing them to feel more comfortable with their wealth.

Does the motivation behind the giving by such people matter as much as the benefit it delivers? Peter Singer thinks not. As he puts it, the parents whose children could die from rotavirus care more about getting the help that will save their children's lives than about the motivations of those who make that possible.[1]

THE GIVING PLEDGE

In 2010, Bill and Melinda Gates and Warren Buffet launched the Giving Pledge, which is described as a simple concept: an open invitation for billionaires, or those who would be if not for their giving, to publicly dedicate the majority of their wealth to philanthropy. Since that time over 170 pledges have been made by individuals and couples, from 21 countries, ranging in age from 30 to 90. Each signatory has an opportunity to write a letter explaining their reasons for giving and their intentions. These letters vary considerably in length and detail, and provide an excellent insight into the philanthropic motives of wealthy benefactors. The letters were analysed using Leximancer, a content analysis software tool, that identifies key concepts and their connectedness, removing any preconceptions and biases from the researcher.[2] Results from this analysis are shown in Figs. 2.1 and 2.2.

This figure tells a simple story. Philanthropy is used to transfer money the wealthy have accumulated to help other groups and people, aided and supported by research. Figure 2.2 displays the same data in a different way.

These data include the diversity of motivations behind the Giving Pledge, but in aggregate tell a common story—in some ways a template—for the reasons for giving. The first element in the template—and almost ubiquitous in the Pledges—is acknowledgement of the importance

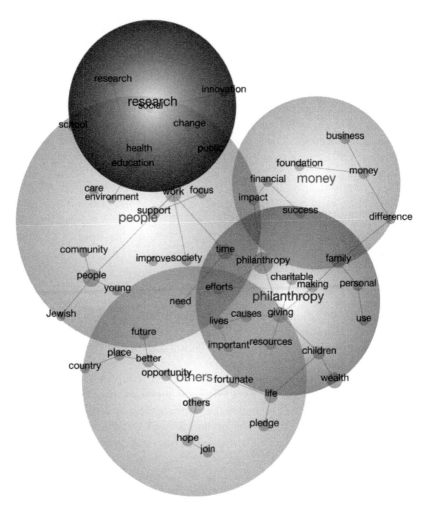

Fig. 2.1   Leximancer analysis of Giving Pledges

of family. This includes the influence that parents had on the donors' philanthropic beliefs. Hong Kong philanthropist James Chen says his father's philanthropic spirit inspires him every day. It also addresses donors' children, commonly a desire to involve them in philanthropic work or to prevent them from having to deal with the burdens of great wealth. Mark

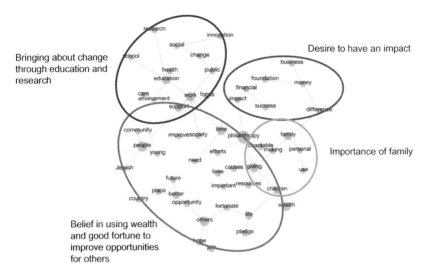

Bringing about change through education and research

Desire to have an impact

Importance of family

Belief in using wealth and good fortune to improve opportunities for others

Fig. 2.2 Interpretation of Leximancer analysis of Giving Pledge

Zuckerberg and Priscilla Chan in "A letter to our daughter" describe how the birth of their child was the stimulus to their giving.[3] The second element is a strong belief in using wealth—and many admit to how fortune dealt them a good hand—to improve opportunities for others. Notably this is not a simple transfer of funds to assist with existing problems, but means by which opportunities are created in communities, and for young people in particular, to improve their lot. The third element is the keen desire to have an impact: they wish to use their funds to maximum effect. The fourth element is the concern to bring about innovation and change through education and research, with a dedication to schools, universities and healthcare.

RELIGION

Philanthropy has played an important role in defining and sustaining many religions, and there is a strong religious motivation underlying the giving of many philanthropists. Although faith-based giving has declined in some Western nations, it still remains significant and is centrally important in Islam and Buddhism. Major religions encourage giving, for example as Judeo-Christian Tithes, Islamic Zakat and Buddist

Dāna. Baroness Rabbi Julia Neuberger, previously CEO of the King's Fund, a UK charity supporting healthcare, argues in these faiths such contributions are more than simply giving to alleviate social problems and are also contributions to social justice: to evening up injustices and the cards one was dealt. Giving ten per cent of your income, she argues, is not about generosity, but a form of religious duty.[4]

John Wesley neatly captured the Protestant work ethic when he sermonized about the need to gain all you can, save all you can and give all you can. Much philanthropy in eighteenth- and nineteenth-century Britain was inseparable from donors' Christianity. John D. Rockefeller Snr. and John Templeton went so far as to claim their money was given to them by god.

Muslims have supported the poor through philanthropy for centuries. The Koran advises wealthy people to give away a portion of their wealth and refers to the importance of meeting the basic needs of the poor and needy. Under Islamic law, an owner of property can bequeath it and its income by legal endowment (the *waqf* system) to particular beneficiaries or causes. In this way philanthropic causes, such as poverty alleviation, are perpetually endowed.

In addition to faith-based foundations, some secular foundations have strong religious influences. The Kings Fund in the UK, for example, automatically has the Bishop of London and Chief Rabbi on its Council.

Julia Neuberger argues faith-based philanthropy should look for the neediest, tend them with love, raise money and persuade others to contribute, and have no agenda to convert anyone to their faith.

There was, however, no shortage of evangelizing and moralizing from the great American philanthropists of the past. Andrew Carnegie's dictum about he who dies rich dies disgraced, was circumscribed by his harsh distinction between giving to the deserving and undeserving. The former are in need because, despite their industrious efforts, circumstances have conspired against them; the latter deserve no support because of their bad decisions. Carnegie fulminated against giving money to "the slothful, the drunken, the unworthy", believing those who gave to such undeserving promotes an evil "moral infection" of more and more people becoming dependent on donations. Recognizing the difficulties in distinguishing the deserving from the undeserving, he recommended that philanthropists dedicate their efforts to finding ways of doing so. He himself decided that rather than provide for the needy directly his support would go to libraries, meeting halls, hospitals and universities. To encourage religiosity through the uplifting effect of music, he purchased 7500 organs for churches. Carnegie's views on charity were bombastic. "It would be better to throw money into the sea than to give it to charity", he wrote. While there is much to admire in the generosity of benefactors such as Carnegie, moralizing self-righteousness is never likely to be popular. Its most extreme manifestation is disturbingly captured in the religious cant found in Robert Tressell's classic novel *The Ragged-Trousered Philanthropists.*

Other philanthropists keen to push their beliefs on their beneficiaries include George Peabody who built affordable housing for poor working people in London in the mid-nineteenth century, but insisted on a night-time curfew and a strict moral code. The deeply religious oil baron, J. Howard Pew, fought against the church's promotion of secular causes, such as birth control or opposition to capital punishment, and distributed Hayek's *Road to Serfdom* to clergymen. In the 1950s, Howard Pew funded evangelical preacher Billy Graham to counter liberal philosophies (Sparks 2016). Hayek's own views on philanthropy were recognition of the valuable contribution it makes compared to the State, but wariness of any moral imperative to do visible good for others which he considered irreconcilable with the open societies to which people owe their wealth.

Although diminishing in importance, religious affiliation influences giving in the West. A 2015 national poll of 1000 people by the Philanthropy Roundtable in the USA found 34% cited their main contributions being to religious causes; the next highest was medical at 14%. Another estimate by Zinsmeister (2016) estimates 39% of US donations go to religions. Religion does not appear to be, however, a motivation behind the giving of major philanthropists such as Bill and Melinda Gates and Warren Buffett.

There remains wide diversity in the motivations and aims of philanthropists, with support offered to the most conservative and most liberal and socially progressive causes. They generously and passionately fund pro- and anti-abortion campaigns, support environmental movements and the mining and oil industries, and are attracted and appalled by government involvement in a wide range of issues from education to science. David Callahan's (2017) view is the wealthy nowadays really are different from other Americans in their ideology. "They are more fiscally conservative and socially liberal than the population as a whole. They have a stronger belief in market solutions and technocratic fixes".

Choosing what to support is affected by factors such as philanthropists' interests, values, political opinions and personality. The personalities can be very strong-willed and perhaps a little immune to irony. Many hold dear the idea that they are always capable of making better decisions than governments. Some generous philanthropists energetically avoid paying tax, others donate to the arts, science and education while decrying public investment in them. While some may revel in the attention they receive as benefactors, philanthropists are not necessarily ego-driven. Callahan reports that in the USA between 2005 and 2015, there have been at least ten philanthropic gifts of $100 million or more that have been made anonymously.

Effective altruism

Effective altruism is the name of a movement that began in the 2000s, often associated with the philosopher Peter Singer. Part philosophy, part social movement, it is held to be particularly attractive to Millennials. Its concerns lie with having evidence of the impact of giving in areas that most accord with givers' values. Or, as one of its leading advocates puts it: "effective altruism is the project of using evidence and reason to figure out how to benefit others as much as possible, and taking action on that basis... Its aims are welfarist, impartial, and maximising: effective altruists aim to maximise the wellbeing of all" (MacAskill 2017). Its causes include alleviating poverty in the developing world and animal suffering.

The concept of effective altruism is applied broadly to any initiatives that benefit people, and is therefore more extensive in scope than the definition of philanthropy adopted in this book. Its practical manifestations include *Giving What We Can*,[5] an organization where individuals pledge at least 10% of their income throughout their working lives, and *80,000 Hours*,[6] an organization that advises people on careers that have positive social impact.

The movement has faced criticisms, mainly associated with its assumptions about "effectiveness". Its attempts to compare and then prioritize the relative importance of causes, and the weighting of very different challenging and pressing problems, in order to "maximise" impact is always likely to be controversial. What is the ranking of caring for a sick child in Swaziland compared to Switzerland? A person giving to a cause to which they are deeply emotionally attached may be more effective to them than giving a larger amount to a cause which experts claim has more evidence of impact, but is less meaningful to the donor. Effective altruism also assumes that there is sufficient evidence of impact to inform which interventions are more positive, when outcomes may be contingent on unrelated factors.

THE QUESTION OF TAX

There is much debate about whether and how tax incentives increase philanthropic giving. Charitable giving has been tax exempt in the USA since 1917. Donations are more or less tax free as are the returns from investing endowments built up through donations. The issue of tax concessions to philanthropic and charitable giving is contentious and continuing. On the one hand is the view that by reducing tax liabilities on giving the state is to an extent incentivizing and subsidizing benefactions. As it is forsaking tax revenues it therefore has a right to influence how that money is spent. On the other hand, is the view that private donors should be entitled to spend their wealth as they like without any interference from the government. Tax deductibility in this view is less an incentive for the giver and more a benefit to the receiver. As the beneficiary is the public good, there should be no tax burden.

Critics of the present arrangements, such as Skocpol (2016), argue the US government has given enormous tax benefits to wealthy philanthropists: "magnifying the impact of their values and choices in public affairs". And Robert Reich (2013) argues that philanthropy in the USA has long involved subsidizing the exercise of individual liberty. He also points out that philanthropy occurred prior to the introduction of tax incentives. On the other hand, proponents, such as Alex Reid (2016), argue the income tax exemptions are more important than simple tax rules, but "form a vital legal boundary between the state and civil society. They are not subsidies for civil society, but rather fences that keep government from interfering in a sector that is vital to our national freedom".

In their search to progress their favoured causes, it is in the philanthropists' interests to maximize their resources and freedom to operate when constructing their mechanisms for giving. Mark Zuckerberg and Priscilla Chan's Chan Zuckerberg Initiative is a new limited liability company which directs their giving and is not subject to the same disclosure rules as foundations. Some of Zuckerberg's plans for maintaining control through novel shareholding structures became unstuck. While not referring to this particular instance, the ambition of some philanthropists is to give their cake away and keep it too.

Given the contentious nature of some political or issues-based giving, it is worth reflecting on the views of Chuck Collins (2016), the Oscar Meyer heir, who argues that governments should establish two types of charitable entities and give them different tax benefits. Donations to groups that "alleviate poverty, reduce inequality, and address urgent social problems" would be fully deductible; other donations would not get the full benefit. Peter Singer says the only true philanthropy is that given to the poor.

The question of which philanthropic organizations should receive tax benefits remains vexatious. In the UK, Eton College, one of the world's most privileged and expensive schools, is a registered charity and thus receives tax relief. Then there is the distinction between different kinds of activity within the same organization. Should a church-based organization's spending on converting more adherents be treated the same way as its spending on social causes?

It remains a serious and open question of whether the motivation of some philanthropic giving, especially through the form of donor-advised funds, resides less with the altruism or social or moral conscience of the giver, and more with a simple question of tax minimization. The construction of the most effective tax regime for giving is also a continuing question. Although tax issues remain very germane for many givers, over time the level of giving in the USA has remained relatively stable during fluctuations in tax rates. Tax deductions are only available to those who itemize deductions on tax returns, and so those with low income get no advantages, and deductions and hence benefits increase the higher the levels of income.

Especially insightful is a 2016 Report by the Charities Aid Foundation that found no correlation between tax rates and the proportion of GDP spent by individuals in 24 nations representing over half of the world's population and 75% of the global economy. The report looked at measures including overall tax burden, top tax rate, average income tax, corporation tax, government expenditure as a percentage of GDP and employer social security charges. The lack of correlation between government spending, income tax or corporation tax and giving points to the dangers of simplistic assumptions about the motivations behind philanthropy. As the Report notes we attempt to simplify our conception of what constitutes an enabling environment for giving at our peril. It points to the importance of culture and tradition, religiosity, political history, the rule of law, trust in institutions and the regulation of charities and the legal environment for civil society activism, amongst other factors, that affect the propensity of people to give (Charity Aid Foundation 2016).

NOTES

1. Peter Singer, "What Should a Billionaire Give—And What Should You?", *New York Times Magazine*, December 17, 2006.
2. www.leximancer.com.
3. https://www.facebook.com/notes/mark-zuckerberg/a-letter-to-our-daughter/10153375081581634/.
4. https://podcasts.apple.com/gb/podcast/philanthropy-faith-and-public-policy/id1031164056?i=1000358724873.
5. https://www.givingwhatwecan.org/.
6. https://80000h.org/.

REFERENCES

Acs, Z. (2013). *Why Philanthropy Matters*. Princeton, NJ: Princeton University Press.

Callahan, D. (2017). *The Givers: Wealth, Power, and Philanthropy in a New Gilded Age*. New York: Knopf.

Charities Aid Foundation. (2016). *Gross Domestic Philanthropy*. https://www.cafonline.org/about-us/blog-home/giving-thought/how-giving-works/gross-domestic-philanthropy.

Collins, C. (2016). *Born on Third Base*. White River Junction, VT: Chelsea Green Publishing.

Crocker, R. (2005). "Nothing More for Men's Colleges": The Educational Philanthropy of Mrs. Russell Sage. In A. Walton (Ed.), *Women and Philanthropy in Education*. Bloomington: Indiana University Press.

Dodgson, M., & Gann, D. (2018). *The Playful Entrepreneur: How to Survive and Thrive in an Uncertain World*. New Haven and London: Yale University Press.

Freeman, M. (2013). Quakers, Business and Philanthropy. In S. Angell & B. Dandelion (Eds.), *The Oxford Handbook of Quaker Studies*. Oxford: Oxford University Press.

Geddes Poole, A. (2014). *Philanthropy and the Construction of Victorian Women's Citizenship: Lady Frederick Cavendish Miss Emma Cons*. Toronto: University of Toronto Press.

Jeffreys, E., & Allatson, P. (2015). *Celebrity Philanthropy*. Bristol: Intellect.

MacAskill, W. (2017). Effective Altruism: Introduction. *Essays in Philosophy, 18*(1), 1. https://doi.org/10.7710/1526-0569.1580.

Mayer, J. (2016). *Dark Money: How a Secretive Group of Billionaires Is Trying to Buy Political Control in the US*. Melbourne: Scribe Publications.

McClain, M. (2017). *Ellen Browning Scripps: New Money and American Philanthropy*. Lincoln: University of Nebraska.

Ostrower, F. (1997). *Why the Wealthy Give: The Culture of Elite Philanthropy*. Princeton, NJ: Princeton University Press.

Perkins, A. (2011). *Edwin Rogers Embree: The Julius Rosenwald Fund, Foundation Philanthropy, and American Race Relations*. Bloomington: Indiana University Press.

Prochaska, F. (1990). Philanthropy. In F. Thompson (Ed.), *The Cambridge Social History of Britain* (pp. 1750–1950). Cambridge: Cambridge University Press.

Reich, R. (2013, March/April). What Are Foundations For? *Boston Review*.

Reid, A. (2016). Why Is Charitable Activity Tax Protected? In Zinsmeister, K. (2016). How Philanthropy Fuels American Success. In *The Almanac of American Philanthropy*. Washington, DC: Philanthropy Roundtable.

Schervish, P. (2003, November 14). *Hyperagency and High-Tech Donors: A New Theory of the New Philanthropists*. New Haven: Boston College Social Welfare Research Institute.

Shapiro, R. (2018). Asian Philanthropy Explained. In R. Shapiro, M. Mirchandani, & H. Jang (Eds.), *Pragmatic Philanthropy: Asian Charity Explained*. Singapore: Palgrave Macmillan.

Shirley, S. (2012). *Let IT Go*. Andrews, UK.

Singer, P. (2015). *The Most Good You Can Do: How Effective Altruism Is Changing Ideas About Living Ethically*. New Haven: Yale University Press.

Skocpol, T. (2016). Politics Symposium: Why Political Scientists Should Study Organized Philanthropy. *PS Political Science and Politics, 49*(3), 433–436.

Sparks, E. (2016). J. Howard Pew. In Zinsmeister, K. (2016). How Philanthropy Fuels American Success. In *The Almanac of American Philanthropy*. Washington, DC: Philanthropy Roundtable.

Zinsmeister, K. (2016). How Philanthropy Fuels American Success. In *The Almanac of American Philanthropy*. Washington, DC: Philanthropy Roundtable.

CHAPTER 3

Philanthropy and Innovation

Abstract This chapter examines the close relationships between philanthropy and innovation. A case study of philanthropy improving eyesight in Africa is provided. The crucial impact of philanthropy on science and universities is discussed. A case study of how philanthropy fundamentally changed Queensland University is provided. The intimate relationship between philanthropy and the arts is explored. A case study is provided of the impact of philanthropy on a major arts institution. The connections between philanthropy and social and humanitarian innovation is described.

Keywords Philanthropy and innovation · Philanthropy and science · Philanthropy and universities · Philanthropy and the arts · Philanthropy and social innovation · Philanthropy and humanitarian innovation

CHALLENGING THE STATUS QUO

Lord Beveridge's report (Beveridge 1942) that led to the creation of the welfare state in Britain—which replaced traditional reliance on patronage and charity in many areas of public life—was very aware of the importance of philanthropy. He emphasized how it "breaks routines" and finds "fresh channels for action", providing a crucial adjunct to the activities

© The Author(s) 2020
M. Dodgson and D. Gann, *Philanthropy,
Innovation and Entrepreneurship,*
https://doi.org/10.1007/978-3-030-38017-5_3

of governments and a necessary source of pluralism in society. Our definition of innovation is similar, it involves novelty and disruption to the status quo, and can occur in a wide range of activities (Dodgson et al. 2014; Dodgson 2017).

Whether observers of philanthropy have a "hope of the future" or "fifth column" view, or come from the left or right of politics, one thing they tend to agree with is that philanthropy is a potential source of innovation.

Nielsen (2002) says philanthropy offers:

> ...unique freedom from the dependence on other institutions on markets or constituencies that cripple their capacity to take the long-term view and bring a competent and disinterested approach to the search for (solutions to) complex problems.

As well as taking the long view, philanthropy provides the opportunity to:

> back a promising but unproven idea, individual or institution; to take an unpopular or unorthodox stand; to facilitate change... to act and not merely react; to initiate, even to gamble and dare.

The world is confronted by numerous complex and challenging ("wicked") problems (Rittel and Weber 1973), that require long-term, innovative and risky approaches to finding solutions. Short-term electoral cycles, and pressures on government finances and associated scrutiny of public expenditures, constrains the innovative and risk-taking abilities of the public sector. Failures in policy initiatives are damaging to politicians and career-limiting to public servants, so become unacceptable. Experiments, new explorations, new thinking become proscribed. Well-established institutions and interest groups become so deeply embedded in polity and society that they can become obstacles to innovation. Corporations, often hampered by financial market short-termism, are also increasingly unable to address these problems—to innovate by breaking routines and finding fresh channels—in meaningful ways. Philanthropy can fill this void, adding to its societal significance. Helmut Anheier and Diana Leat (2006) introduce the concept of "creative philanthropy", based on creativity and innovation, and which can take risks that other elements in society cannot. Warren Buffett calls philanthropy "society's risk capital".

Philanthropy therefore has the potential to overcome the status quo and compensate for the myopia of the institutions of government and business. It can question orthodoxy and encourage innovative new approaches to problems and it can do so much more quickly and responsively than governments, tied as they are to lengthy and highly politicized decision-making processes and demanding compliance requirements. Not being tied to short electoral or financial reporting cycles, philanthropy can adopt more long-term and consistent investments. As philanthropy can fund numerous and divergent approaches to problems it increases the competition between ideas and their contestability, heightening the ability to find effective answers to problems in evolving and uncertain circumstances.

Social innovation and philanthropy

A small, but growing, body of the innovation literature refers to "social" innovation (e.g. Mulgan et al. 2007). This includes socially innovative organizations, such as Greenpeace and the Open University, public campaigns, such as those preventing dangerous driving, and individuals, such as Muhammed Yunus, founder of the Grameen Bank, with its microloans. Such social innovation is often the target of philanthropy. The Gates' Foundation, for example, with its focus on health and poverty alleviation, and concern for how scientific and technological innovation can assist these objectives, is aiming for social innovation. Such foundations recognizes, however, that social change is massively complex, involving interactions and interdependencies between social and political as well as economic and technological innovations. Those social innovations which lead to social progress are, furthermore, understood to most commonly result from the interaction of a variety of organizations and institutions: government, private sector, NGOs and social entrepreneurs and enterprises.

As Mulgan et al. (2007) point out, the factors that encourage social innovation are often similar to those that promote innovation in the private sector, including: innovation-supporting leaders; specific sources of finance; empowered, incentivized and well-trained innovative individuals; R&D tailored to particular challenges and contexts; and incubators for new ideas. They also refer to the: "critical role played by the 'connectors' in any innovation system—the brokers, entrepreneurs and institutions that link together people, ideas, money and power". Philanthropy can make a powerful contribution to social innovation by supporting such intermediaries.

The question arises about which kinds of philanthropy best funds innovation? Long-established foundations may themselves become very conservative and risk-adverse. Nielsen, writing of foundations in the 1980s, was sceptical, seeing many of them as timid and unimaginative. A 2011 article in the *Economist* on the centenary celebrations of both the Carnegie Foundation and IBM, argued that when it came to "making the world better", the foundation made the greater contribution for the first 50 years, but the company, including through its work with government, had the greater impact in their second half-century.[1] It suggests that foundations become conservative over time and also noted IBM's corporate philanthropy now exceeds that of the Carnegie Foundation.

When seeking innovation one often looks to the role of entrepreneurs, because they are used to risk and opportunity seeking. A great number of contemporary philanthropists have accumulated their wealth through their innovations in the technology and financial sectors. But are entrepreneur philanthropists best placed to understand the complexities and machinations of the interactions of people and institutions needed to further social change? And should businesses and entrepreneurs set the agenda and define investment priorities around social issues? To what extent do the public have a say in the way businesses or wealthy individuals create public goods? How clear are the motivations of philanthropists and how transparent is their influence? These are questions to which we shall return, but here we offer a case of where a businessman has used innovation to great effect.

Case Study: Being Patient and Seeing Clearly

According to one estimate, 2.5 billion people around the world lack access to spectacles, 1.1 billion of whom need glasses to improve their near vision. This is mainly a problem in the developing world. As the world's population grows and ages, these numbers are set to grow significantly. The disadvantage this causes individual sufferers and their families, and the negative impact it has on communities and economic productivity, is immense. Numbers of philanthropic foundations are addressing various aspects of the problem. The World Health Organization (WHO) estimates that 33% of visual impairment is caused by cataracts.[2] The Fred Hollows Foundation offers cheap operations to replace cataracts, and trains surgeons and nurses and manufactures cheap lens in countries such as Nepal. The WHO estimates that 43% of impairment is caused by uncorrected refractive errors, such as myopia or astigmatism. Adlens is a social enterprise that makes and sells assistive devices to deal with these errors.

Working with health agencies in the countries concerned, it has sold over 600,000 pairs of adjustable focus glasses at US$1.50 a pair in developing nations such as Rwanda.

The co-founder of Adlens, James Chen, has developed an approach to his giving that he describes as patient and audacious (Chen 2017). The patient aspects of such an approach takes risks for long-term social rewards, recognizing that sometimes solutions to problems can require dedicated commitment for a generation. James believes that the virtues of philanthropy—discipline, dedication, fidelity—sometimes requires "deep time" to realize. Audacious philanthropy, he contends, goes well beyond the writing of big cheques: it matches real money to real purpose, and real change. Change, he argues, requires resilience and determination.

With a background as an investor in Hong Kong, James Chen and his wife Su Lee established the Chen Yet Sen Family Foundation in 2003 in honour of James's late father, with a focus on early childhood literacy and building libraries. It funded initiatives such as the Hong Kong chapter of Bring Me a Book, and the Feng Zikai Chinese Children's Picture Book Award. The Foundation has been driven by the desire to bring a new reading culture across Greater China, and encourages parents to read aloud to children and offers parent and teacher training. It is driven by a belief that parents reading to their children strengthen family bonds and encourage a culture of learning. Now an independent organization, Bring Me a Book Hong Kong has thousands of volunteers and training hours completed, and 400 libraries installed in schools and organizations throughout the city. James has also supported the establishment of the Stone Soup Happy Reading Alliance, which now has a collective of 26 schools in China.

In 2004, James learnt about the new technology of variable focus lenses, and requiring glasses himself immediately recognized how helpful it could be in developing countries. He had lived all around the world, and had grown up for a period in Nigeria, so was sensitive to the contemporary challenges of poorer nations. Variable focus lenses can be manually adjusted to an individual's near, intermediate or distance vision needs. The curvature of the lenses in the spectacles is altered by filling them with liquid and allowing the wearer to vary their power with a simple dial. They were invented by Professor Joshua Silver from the Department of Atomic and Laser Physics at Oxford University, and he joined James as a co-founder of Adlens. The company currently employs over 70 staff in five locations around the world, and is the largest manufacturer of variable focus eyewear. James says that developing the technology and building the company towards a sustainable state took a decade.

Part of the motivation for his ways of working in this area lay with his frustration with governments and development agencies. He was exasperated, for instance, in the way the World Bank funds adult literacy classes in sub-Saharan Africa but doesn't address the endemic vision losses in those aged over 35 in the region. How, he asked, can you read if you can't see? At a Rockefeller conference with world development agency executives he became dismayed at their continual allegiance to state-aided large government projects. James, in contrast, believes in bottom-up approaches, and in individual enterprise, and this is seen in the way he created Adlens as a company and the way that people pay for their glasses. They are not free and are therefore valued more.

As part of his strategy of bringing the glasses to developing nations, the Vision for a Nation organization was launched in 2010, to help health ministries in low-income countries build primary eye care services. Initially targeting Rwanda, its nationwide programme includes three-day vision assessment training for nurses, which is now being incorporated into the curriculum of all the country's eight nursing schools. It has trained over 2700 nurses, supported by the nation's network of 45,000 community health workers, increasing public awareness of the affordable availability of eye care. By 2017, around 1.6 million Rwandans received a screening, with 350,000 receiving glasses and 325,000 referred for specialist treatment. Rwanda now has universal access to vision correction.

Upon entry into Rwanda, James was deeply sceptical about working with the government, but an effective partnership has been built, and he is full of praise for the Rwandan government and its department of health, which have been completely supportive. Having demonstrated its value, more traditional donors are supporting the efforts, with, for example, the UK's Department for International Development offering funding. James now actively supports and promotes collaboration and partnerships with governments and other organizations.

In 2018, it was announced that a $1 billion Vision Catalyst Fund was to be established under the auspices of the Queen Elizabeth Diamond Jubilee Trust to "provide vision to entire populations across the Commonwealth". Involving companies, such as Standard Chartered, UBS and the ophthalmic optic firm Essilor, non-government organizations, such as Fred Hollows Foundation and Clearly, and the International Agency for the Prevention of Blindness, it aims to raise the Fund in two years with the objective of providing sustainable and efficient long-term solutions to eye health. James Chen committed $10 million to the fund.

James considers his philosophy accords well with the characteristics of Chinese philanthropy. He was very influenced by the approach of his father and grandfather, who taught him the importance of philanthropy and getting involved with its benefaction. His approach to philanthropy, James argues, complements the Chinese approach because it shares two fundamental Confucian tenets: a family focus as the primary source of giving and means of inculcating the sense of civic duty; and the long-term view, considering progress over decades rather than years.

On the practice of philanthropy, James says it is difficult enough to earn money, but giving it away so it accomplishes what you want it to do is even harder. Generally speaking, he contends, that if you want to be an effective donor, you need to develop domain expertise. He suggests a challenge of philanthropy is to take more risk, of which there are two kinds: first, being exposed to fraud and incompetence, second, discovering that despite your best efforts they simply did not work. The latter provides an opportunity to learn and improve. His adherence to the principle of audacious philanthropy is seen in his stated ambition: "I want everyone in the world to be able to access affordable glasses and take them for granted".

The concern for continually innovating is seen in the use of technology. James is working with an academic who has designed a proven technique for retina-scanning using a Smartphone. He believes this will revolutionize the way the organizations he works with will operate as eye care can be taken to even the most remote areas and all of the cost and limitations of training nurses and building clinics reduces. James's book, *Clearly*, describes his journey and conveys his objectives for the future. In it he asks about technology: "Will we be able to use drones to drop supplies of glasses to distant places? What role could 3D printers play in crashing the cost of glasses? How close are we to developing eyedrops that correct vision through nanotechnology rather than spectacles? How can we encourage local designers and entrepreneurs to create affordable but attractive frames to break down the stigma of wearing glasses? What is the role of artificial intelligence?" (Chen 2017).

A new initiative has been launched called the Clearly Campaign to engage people and harness new ideas. It offers prizes to entrepreneurs who come up with the best ideas for assisting eyesight. One idea to emerge was to lobby the United Nations to make eyesight a basic right.

One of the methods philanthropy supports social progress is through the medium of social entrepreneurship, such as in the case of Adlens. Like many activities in this field, social entrepreneurship is plagued with definitional problems, but essentially it is the application of entrepreneurship—alertness to opportunity and preparedness to take risks—to bring about significant benefits for society. Social entrepreneurs are philanthropic when their primary purpose is strategic, transformational social change.

Patience is a virtue

Bridgespan, the non-profit affiliate of Bain Consulting, undertook a study of 15 of the world's most successful philanthropic interventions, including polio eradication, tobacco control and the introduction of child car seats, and found:

Success took a long time: nearly 90% of the efforts spanned more than 20 years (with a median of about 45 years).

It frequently entailed government cooperation: 80% required changes to government funding, policies, or actions.

It often necessitated collaboration: nearly 75% involved active coordination amongst key actors across sectors.

And at least 66% featured donors who made one or more philanthropic big bets with gifts of $10 million or more.

Susan Wolf Ditkoff and Abe Grindle (2017).

As William Beveridge noted, philanthropy can be an important source of innovation, a stimulus to and means of exploring novelty and change, and we shall now examine how it contributes to innovation in science and the arts.

The advance of science and the promotion of the arts has relied on philanthropic patronage throughout history. The Royal Society, the world's first and most prestigious scientific fellowship, was established in 1660 with aristocratic, then royal, patronage, and in its early centuries relied on the donations from wealthy individuals to fund its projects and prizes. Shakespeare and Goethe relied heavily on the support of aristocratic patrons. Mark Twain relied on the support of a vice president of Standard Oil. Mozart depended on the patronage of Gottried van

Swieten, Haydn was given a job for life by the Esterházy family, and Tchaikovsky's most productive years were funded by Nadezhda von Meck. Ostrower (1997) says "Signs of the philanthropic involvements of the wealthy are not hard to find. Buildings, programs, and even entire institutions are named for wealthy benefactors. The playbills of many performing arts organizations offer long lists of their donors. In museums, placards next to works of art identify the men and women by whom they were donated. Hospital wings and endowed university chairs carry the names of large contributors".

Callahan (2017) concurs, writing nowadays philanthropists are: "showing up in the arts and sciences, covering the paychecks of molecular biologists, curators, neuroscientists, art conservationists, geneticists, professors holding endowed chairs, and on and on. Pick nearly any disease, and you'll find a deep-pocketed donor who's hot on the trail of a research breakthrough. Name a leading cultural institution, and chances are it's lately received new infusions of cash from billionaire backers. Get lost in a top hospital, and you'll find yourself wandering from one named wing to another. Visit any major university, and it will be hard to find a big building on campus that doesn't bear the name of a mega-donor".

PHILANTHROPY AND SCIENCE

Philanthropy funds scientific institutions, instruments and campaigns. The list of great American universities is populated with the names of their eponymous founding benefactors, including Stanford, Carnegie and Mellon, Duke, Drexel, Rensselaer, and Rockefeller (who as well as Rockefeller University also founded the University of Chicago). Philanthropy has long funded large instruments for astronomy, such as telescopes, and oceanography, such as research vessels, and Alfred Loomis's philanthropy was crucial to the wartime development of radar and the atomic bomb. In medicine, it has funded breakthrough work on the treatment of numerous diseases, and conditions such as schizophrenia, autism, and asthma. Its funding has, for example, helps treat prostate cancer and assisted developing Herceptin for the treatment of breast cancer.

John D. Rockefeller Snr. was a pioneer in the development of systematic, large-scale philanthropy, and was instrumental in creating the field of biomedical research and improving medical training around the world. The Rockefeller Foundation has had many hugely impressive successes. William Schneider (2002) shows how the Foundation affected medical research, education, and public health in Europe, the Soviet Union, and China between World War I and the Cold War. Generally effective, he points to the way major advances were achieved in several countries that did not have a notable history in medical research. Diplomatically, he refers to some circumstances, however, where the Rockefeller Foundation was confronted with "local cultural and political imperatives that reshaped or weakened its objectives". There are other instances when investments did not go to plan. Rockefeller Foundation funded the discoveries of vaccines for Yellow Fever, but its funding of research in the USA did not go smoothly. McGoey (2015) tells the story of Hideyo Noguchi, a Japanese-born bacteriologist at the Rockefeller Institute, who believed he had found a cure for the disease. The Rockefeller Foundation distributed his vaccines and antiserums throughout Latin America and Africa, and Nogochi himself spent time in West Africa. Unfortunately for him, he caught Yellow Fever there and died. His cure was useless and the Foundation had to withdraw the vaccine.

It is useful to calibrate the philanthropic contributions to science compared to those from the government. Two of the major contributors to science discussed below, the Howard Hughes Medical Institute and the Simons Foundation, spend around $1 billion annually. The combined budget for the US National Institute for Health and National Science Foundation exceeds $40 billion (although this is subject to political vagaries, and there have been substantial cuts in recent years). But what matters is not only the quantity of funding but its quality.

A common refrain in the world of science and research is the lack of funding for highly innovative, speculative and risky research. Government funding agencies tend to be conservative, shying away from adventurous methodologies and preferring to support those with proven track records (generally older researchers). Philanthropically supported scientific institutes can overcome some of these shortcomings. Philanthropy is more likely to fund buildings, machines and the innovative ideas of younger, less well-established researchers.

The Howard Hughes Medical Institute (HHMI), for example, employs 2500 people. It awards grants and hosts hundreds of researchers in a modern research complex in Virginia. Their work includes cutting-edge research on biology and neuroscience. Researchers are given full funding for six years, with no demands to teach, apply for grants, or demonstrate how their work can be commercialized. A report for the National Bureau of Economic Research (which was itself started with

philanthropic funds) has studied the research productivity of HHMI compared to researchers working on government-funded research projects
(Murray 2012). It found HHMI tolerates early failure, rewards long-
term success, and gives its appointees great freedom to experiment. In
contrast, it found grantees from the government-funded National Institute of Health are subject to short review cycles, predefined deliverables,
and renewal policies unforgiving of failure. The study furthermore found
that HHMI investigators produced high-impact research publications at
a much higher rate than a control group of similarly-accomplished NIH-
funded scientists. Moreover, the former group was more likely to explore
novel lines of inquiry.

In another indicator of the cutting-edge nature of philanthropically
funded research, Zinsmeister (2016) claims 47 Nobel science prize winners have had significant funding from Rockefeller philanthropy in one
form or another. The Nobel Prizes are themselves another example of
philanthropic contributions to science and the arts. When Alfred Nobel
left his considerable wealth to the creation of these five prizes, much to
the consternation of his family, he wanted to celebrate his lifelong devo-
tion to science and engineering, seen in the prizes for physics, chemistry,
medicine or physiology, his love of literature, and concern for the promotion of peace.

Contemporary foundations that have prioritized scientific investments
include the Simons Foundation, funded by the hedge fund investor Jim
Simons and his wife Marilyn, which in a relatively short period of time has
become one of the leading private funders of basic science in the USA.
The foundation makes grants in four areas: Mathematics and Physical Sciences, Life Sciences, autism research and Education and Outreach. The
foundation also has an internal research division, the Simons Center for
Data Analysis, known as the Flatiron Institute.

The mission of the Ellison Medical Foundation, funded by Larry
Ellison, the founder of Oracle, has been "to support basic biomedical
research, with a focus on understanding how humans and other organisms
age, and on defining the fundamental biological mechanisms that prevent
age-related diseases and disabilities". Notable in its mission statement is
its aim "to stimulate new, creative research approaches that might not be
funded by traditional sources or that has been neglected by existing U.S.
research funding programs".[3] The essential principle of the Foundation is
to fund people, not projects, to find good people, give them money, then
stand back.

Paul Allen, the co-founder of Microsoft, has donated $500 million through the Allen Institute for Brain Science to novel and experimental research in fields such as artificial intelligence and gene editing.[4] Allen had early awareness of the Ebola virus, funding research at Kansas State University in 2009. When the Ebola epidemic struck West Africa in 2014, killing nearly 5000 people, Allen quickly donated $100 million, aiding the dispatch of 500 emergency health workers to the region. This was complemented by significant donations from less well-known African philanthropists.

Although less well-funded, philanthropy also supports the social sciences. Olivia Sage, a woman whose personal generosity was thwarted during her marriage to a less than generous man, but immediately given full reign upon his death in 1906. In short order she gave away $45 million of the $75 million she inherited, helping support the development of social science to study social problems. The Russell Sage Foundation she created was instrumental in improving the professionalization of social work (Crocker 2005).

Some philanthropists have appreciated the business value of the social sciences. David Seim (2013) reports how John D. Rockefeller and his son donated generously to social science research, neither from the desire to change the direction of research, nor from a wholly charitable stance, but because of their desire to explore the role of profitable business within the parameters of government and society. Rockefeller's funding of Chicago University saw a focus on the social science applied to public policy, with one building he funded housing 22 leading policy agencies. The Carnegie Corporation paid for Gunnar Myrdal's 1944 report on "An American Dilemma: The Negro Problem and Modern Democracy", revealing the effect of institutionalized racism.

The changes seen in America, with cuts to government investments in science, and greater scientific philanthropy, has led science journalist William Broad to argue in the *New York Times* that American science is increasingly becoming a private enterprise, and it is worth considering the extent to which this trend affects the university sector.[5]

PHILANTHROPY AND UNIVERSITIES

There is a long tradition of universities receiving financial support from benefactors. Harvard University began its first fundraising campaign in 1643 and, in many ways, has become an extraordinary fundraising machine, receiving by some measures an average of over $3 million a day. Universities in the USA and UK are the main recipients of million dollar/pound gifts from philanthropists. The highest percentage of these come from individuals in the USA (70% in 2015), and foundations in the UK (55% in 2015).[6]

Acs (2013) reminds us that many of today's eminent US universities were founded in the last half of the nineteenth century with money from entrepreneurs. He says philanthropists are typically entrepreneurs and, as such, they tend to value institutions that promote and facilitate entrepreneurial activity—that is, institutions that reward hard work, ambition, and innovation, like the modern American university. In the UK, the philanthropy of foundations, such as Wellcome and Wolfson, has been crucial in supporting science, social science and the humanities. There are Wolfson Colleges at Oxford and Cambridge Universities, and the Wolfson Foundation has supported research and infrastructure in 60 other universities.

Some philanthropic contributions to universities can be extraordinary. In 2014, Gerald Chan and his family gave $350 million to Harvard University's School of Public Health, at the time the largest ever donation to a university. A native of Hong Kong, Chan studied as an engineer, earning two degrees from UCLA, before moving to Harvard in the 1970s to study for his Ph.D. Returning to Hong Kong he started a venture capital and private equity company with his brother. He retained his passion for science. His company was an early investor in Chinese technology companies. He maintained his connections with Harvard, sitting on advisory boards and endowing a Chair, and his Morningside Foundation has made numerous education and science-related philanthropic donations in Hong Kong and China.

The dean of Harvard's School of Public Health is quoted as saying: "Traditionally in public health we've had two career paths: research and public service, Gerald pioneered a third path of going into entrepreneurship and innovation".[7] Chan argues for a new philanthropy in support of public health. He suggests financial capital devoted to the maximization of profits for shareholders hasn't the incentives to support public health, so what is needed is capital where (1) financial returns are negligible, (2) horizons are long term, (3) tolerance for risk is high; and (4) decisions are made by scientists with product development experience. He calls such resources philanthropic capital.

The Chan donation was unrestricted; that is, the money is to be spent in the way the university thinks best. Research in the Chan School of Public Health focuses on pandemics, humanitarian crises, failing health systems and social and environmental threats to health. The money also supports junior researchers in areas that don't qualify for government funding, as well as advanced classrooms and computer resources. Chan's philosophy extols the virtue of learning that strives towards ambitious aims and he is all too aware of the challenges that threaten such purpose. His views are eloquently captured in his Commencement Speech at Harvard in 2012.

> Being flooded with minutiae of everyday life subverts our intellectual life by luring us into, and holding us captive in the present, in what is, such that we have no time and no energy left to consider what might be, or what can be, or what should be. The peril we face in today's society is that we unwittingly become mere pragmatists, and soon, exhausted realists.[8]

He has used his wealth to provide the means for scientists to pursue their ambitions to explore and learn and help make their lives and organization for which they work rich with ideas.

Philanthropy from private foundations and gifts from wealthy individuals has become a core component of the funding of American universities. As a study for the National Bureau of Economic Research shows, philanthropy contributes over $4 billion annually to operations, endowment and buildings devoted to scientific, engineering and medical research. When combined with endowment income, university research funding from science philanthropy is $7 billion a year. This provides almost 30% of the annual research funds in leading universities. Fiona Murray, the author of the report, notes:

> The documented extent of science philanthropy and its strong emphasis on translational medical research raises important questions for Federal policymakers. In determining their own funding strategies, they must no longer assume that their funding is the only source in shaping some fields of research, while recognizing that philanthropy may ignore other important fields. (Murray 2012)

The public policy concerns are wider than this. There are fears about the relative virtues of giving to already extremely wealthy institutions compared to other, struggling, elements of the education system. MIT had an endowment of over $16 billion in 2018, and Stanford University's is even larger. It has an endowment of over $26 billion, and received four gifts of at least $100 million in 2015 alone. It attracted $1.8 billion in gifts in 2018, and a quarter of its annual revenues come from its investment income. The founder of Nike, Phil Knight, donated $400 million to Stanford University in 2016, to be used to cover tuition and living expenses for one hundred graduate students a year. This money flowed into Stanford at the same time as State funding for public universities and community colleges fell. It might be noted that these five gifts exceeded the $600 million attracted by all UK universities from philanthropic donations from trusts and foundations in 2015–2016. Callahan (2017) says America's public universities are today being more heavily shaped by the wealthy than at any time since these institutions were created.

University research and education directly and indirectly underpins America's most successful entrepreneurial companies, and through their philanthropy those entrepreneurs aim to maintain the system that produced their wealth. They do this through giving and through co-locating their headquarters and research facilities nearby leading universities, exemplified by Silicon Valley technology companies around Stanford University. The concern of philanthropists to encourage close interaction between business and industry is by no means a new or exclusively American phenomenon. As a Trustee of the UK's Wolfson Foundation, Lord Solly Zuckerman, was instrumental in creating the Foundation's Technology Projects Scheme in the 1960s: a programme to engage industry and universities in joint development with a highly practical focus.

The nexus of research and entrepreneurship also has altruistic aims. As told by Gerald Chan, The Cystic Fibrosis Foundation, along with the pharmaceutical company Vertex, developed a drug which for the first time provides a cure for Cystic Fibrosis. The Foundation owned the royalty for the drug, and sold it for $3 billion. With these funds, the Foundation can fund genetic characterization of every Cystic Fibrosis patient in the USA as well as the development of drugs that address other mutations of the disease, providing the potential for offering a cure for up to 9 in 10 sufferers.[9]

Philanthropy also underpins some extreme libertarian and right-wing causes that can be accused of being anti-science. The Cato Institute, a think tank originally funded by one of the Koch brothers, has long campaigned for the removal of government funding for science in the belief it "crowds out", and is less effective than, philanthropic and private sector funding. Cato also opposes gun control, compulsory seat belt laws, and anti-smoking legislation.

Highlighting how cautious universities need to be in accepting philanthropic gifts, in 2010 the London School of Economics (LSE) accepted a donation from the Gaddafi Foundation at a time when the Libyan leader's son was alleged to have been awarded a Ph.D. that was ghostwritten and contained plagiarism. In 2011, the LSE came under increased public scrutiny during the Libyan uprising, leading to the resignation of its Director. In 2019, it became public that universities, including Harvard and MIT, had received substantial gifts from a convicted sex offender. In the latter case, it was revealed that the Director of one of MIT's most prominent laboratories had concealed donations from the person concerned. The President of MIT recorded his shame and distress that the university had allowed these donations to elevate the reputation of someone convicted of "horrifying acts". The Director of the Lab resigned.

Despite such high-profile instances, universities have become far more professionalized in their fundraising, and while this has valuably increased the amounts invested in research and education, there remain significant concerns about its implications for their nature and purpose. One concern lies with the increasing "corporatization" of the university, with the managerial practices of business usurping collegiality, and the functions of the university being diverted towards meeting business needs. Another lies with some of the practices being used to identify wealthy alumni as potential donors, sometimes using external "wealth identification services" with questions raised about the protection of alumni privacy. The pursuit of philanthropic donations is also argued to enhance competition between universities, reducing opportunities for the collaboration so necessary for research progress.

One concern about philanthropic donations to universities is that they favour the elite universities. This may have the advantage in ensuring resources are not spread too thinly, supporting great depth in research excellence. But it may also accentuate inequality, disadvantaging universities that contribute more to social mobility. Nonetheless, there are many examples of smaller, regional universities receiving substantial benefactions from wealthy local people with strong allegiance to their home areas.

Philanthropy as Animateur

As those that work within them will attest, significant structural change does not happen easily in universities. The following case shows how skilled philanthropists can assist major new initiatives (Dodgson and Staggs 2012).

In the mid-1990s, the University of Queensland (UQ) embarked on a strategy to significantly expand its scientific research capacity in order to elevate it into the top ranks of international universities. Philanthropy played a crucial role in this transformation. In the course of a decade four research institutes were established addressing biotechnology, nanotechnology, neuroscience and the molecular and cellular basis of disease, raising over $1 billion in investment and employing 1300 staff. The initiative was built upon a supportive government at Federal and State level, ambitious university leadership, and a number of individual academic entrepreneurs. Private philanthropy played a crucial role as *animateur* amongst the contributors.

Key to the establishment of the research institutes was the generosity of Chuck Feeney, of Atlantic Philanthropies. Feeney had made his fortune in Duty Free shops and determined to give it away through his Foundation. Feeney's first philanthropic donations began in 1981 at Cornell University. He has invested considerably in his ancestral home: providing substantial support to all seven universities in the Republic of Ireland and two in Northern Ireland. Feeney's Atlantic Philanthropies also invested $220 million in Vietnam between 1998 and 2006. By 2020 it is estimated that the foundation will have given $7.6 billion.

Based on the success of his model in Ireland and Vietnam, Feeney began to look for opportunities in Australia. In Brisbane, he used his friend, former tennis great Ken Fletcher, to "be a kind of spotter to look for opportunities and bring them to our attention" (O'Clery 2007, p. 257). While Feeney's approach was to liaise with somebody with knowledge of the country who would survey the landscape for him and suggest investment ideas when an opportunity presented itself, Atlantic Philanthropies thereafter carefully assessed the proposal. "His philanthropy was opportunistic but he didn't give randomly. He investigated and scrutinized and sometimes tested the people involved with small initial grants. It always came down to his instincts about the quality of the people involved" (O'Clery 2007, p. 245).

In UQ's case, Atlantic Philanthropies' support only came after Feeney brought in a team that probed researchers and administrators with questions about how the Institutes would develop. As one observer noted: "While Feeney was on board with it was his financial guy that we needed to keep happy". Feeney's role was not simply to provide funds. His advocacy and negotiating skills, along with UQ's Vice Chancellor's, proved essential in leveraging funds from Commonwealth and State. Philanthropy operated within a set of fecund but not necessarily well-connected conditions.

The contribution of great philanthropists to university formation is well-known. Less well-known are the changes that can be encouraged within universities through the astute and strategic investment of foundations concerned not with short-term commercial or political payoffs, but with a strategic view of what a university and government can achieve by working together. In this case, a philanthropic organization had sufficient will and resources to help a University cut through significant organizational and political inertia. By 2010 Feeney had donated around $250 million dollars to UQ, but the leverage it negotiated—to $1 billion—was crucial in producing the scale of activities that emerged. Feeney's genius also lies in the way that all the parties involved claim ownership of the initiative. UQ is now often ranked in the top 50 universities in the world.

This example illustrates the transformative power of philanthropy, which can, of course, apply with recipients other than universities. Ideas emerge when good relationships are established, and partners share a vision and embrace a common strategy and mission. Great benefit derives from engaging with visionary philanthropists, where partnerships based on shared values can stimulate new ideas and directions. Mohammed Abdul Latif Jameel's gift to his alma mater MIT not only provided the financial means for the Abdul Latif Jameel World Water and Food Security Lab, but built upon Jameel's expertise and vision in energy, technology and big data to help address global challenges in food and water distribution. Effective philanthropy is commonly more than transactional and thrives on the basis of strong and continuing relationships.

In India, a number of private universities are being created by philanthropists, often with the aim of meeting the demand for technology skills. Ashoka University, which was launched from donations from 101 benefactors, is taking a very different and innovative approach. Concerned at the technocratic nature of Indian universities, and in some case the datedness of their curricula, its founders are attempting to transform the higher education system by creating a liberal arts university. Ashoka University, which accepted its first undergraduates in 2014, aims to be research-intensive and encouraging of independent thought in its students, which are planned eventually to number around 5000. The founders were very concerned to maintain academic freedom, independent from the influence of government or from single powerful benefactors, so it developed a collective governance model, where donors are limited to one position on its Board. To encourage access from all parts of Indian society, around 60% of students receive some form of scholarship. The three major founders of Ashoka are all successful Indian entrepreneurs, and their ambition is not to feed talent into their companies, but to benefit the whole of Indian society by encouraging independent thought amongst people prepared to question those in power.

PHILANTHROPY AND THE ARTS

Philanthropy supports music performance and creation, museums, architecture, film, dance, TV and theatre, libraries, history preservation and conservation, literature and poetry. It sustains excellence in the arts, creates resources for experimentation and innovation, and helps widen participation. Through funding for universities, it supports research in the humanities. While funding the arts may not so immediately address the "finalities" of problems in the same ways as giving to other areas, it enlightens and communicates our understanding of the world, and supports imaginative and innovative initiatives.

There are numerous major cultural entities built by their eponymous philanthropist founders, including the: Smithsonian Museum; Carnegie Hall; Guggenheim Museums in New York, Bilbao and Abu Dhabi; Fick Collection; Juilliard School music conservatory; Pulitzer Prizes for journalism, literature (with separate prizes for novels, plays, biographies, histories), poetry, music composition and photography; Pritzker Prize that commonly awards modernist architects and Driehaus Prize that goes to more classical architectural styles.

Museums have always benefitted from private benefaction. The Uffizi Gallery in Florence was founded in 1581 with the collections of the de Medici family. The British Museum was established in 1753, based largely on the collections of the physician and scientist Sir Hans Sloane. Rich businessmen played crucial roles as donors and trustees in the formation of the UK's National Gallery and National Portrait Gallery. As well as creating these significant international institutions, private philanthropy contributes more locally. In the 1940s, the French philanthropists John and Dominique de Menil began a campaign in Houston, Texas to educate the public and fund and exhibit artists. They promoted modern art, with an especial interest in the Surrealists, and insisted that no admission charges are made, and the Menil Gallery is home to one of the greatest collections of modernist art.

New York's Museum of Modern Art was funded by the Rockefellers and has received some extraordinary donations from philanthropists. In 1991, the media mogul Walter Annenberg donated his collection of impressionist paintings. It was valued at the time at more than a billion dollars. In 2013, Leonard Lauder, CEO of Estée Lauder, donated his collection of cubist work to the Metropolitan Museum of Art, including work by Picasso and Braque. It was also valued at more than a billion dollars.

Concerned that men dominate the funding, governance, and exhibits in art galleries and museums, women philanthropists have created a number of spaces to better represent the contributions of women artists (Blair 2005). Wilhelmina Cole Holladay, for example, founded the National Museum of Women in the Arts in Washington, DC. This museum, which claims to be the only major museum dedicated solely to women's art, provides a range of activities and services.

The National Museum of Women in the Arts
Displays and preserves a collection of more than 5000 objects.
Presents ten exhibitions featuring women artists each year.
Runs a public programs initiative highlighting the power of women and the arts as catalysts for change.
Offers education curricula and programs for learners of all ages.
Maintains a 17,500-volume library and research centre.
Serves as a leading resource for information about gender disparity in the arts.
Highlights women artists on its website, blog and social media channels.
Publishes art history books and a triannual magazine.
Sponsors twenty national and international outreach committees, whose members serve as ambassadors and advocate for artists in their regions.

In the USA, philanthropy has preserved and protected some of its most important historical buildings and monuments, such as Arlington Cemetery, Thomas Jefferson's home at Monticello, Carnegie Hall, Washington Memorial and the Statue of Liberty.

Half of the income for US symphony orchestras is estimated comes from donations. And philanthropy has made music accessible to more people, beginning with the first-ever radio broadcasts from the San Francisco Symphony in 1926. As well as promoting and preserving classical music, philanthropy also supports folk and jazz music and the collection of negro spirituals.

With musical instruments being so expensive—a Stradivarius violin can cost several million dollars—some wealthy individuals and organizations buy then lend them to musicians. By lending the instruments, benefactors with interests in the arts can build relationships with performers, enjoying privileged and even private recitals. Numbers of philanthropic organizations lend instruments for all levels of talent, from the Stradivari Society to the Amati Foundation and Benslow Scheme.[10]

Belief in the importance of the arts and the need for the wealthy to support them is personified in the life of John Maynard Keynes. The great economist, and skilled investor, brought all his financial skills and personal wealth to the service of the arts. Immersed in the world of literature as a member of the Bloomsbury Group from the time he was a student, his marriage to a Russian ballerina surrounded him with more artists. He believed the arts were crucial for the social and cultural values he espoused, and furthermore, in line with his view about how technological progress would reduce the working week, he believed the arts would prepare the new society for a life of leisure and prosperity. Keynes was very conscious of the struggle of artists to fund themselves, arguing they need economic security and enough income, and then be left to themselves. He contributed to a number of schemes to provide more funding to painters, was active in creating the Cambridge Arts Theatre, promoted the preserving of monuments, and was a crucial contributor to the formation of the UK's Arts Council (Upchurch 2016).

Opera Companies: Not just for the "Elite"?

The following case illustrates the manner in which philanthropic funding supports adventurous artistic endeavours and offers them to a broader audience. It provides details on the efforts required to attract and disperse funds from donors.

Based in rural Sussex, the Glyndebourne opera house and company has the motto: "Not the best that we can do but the best that can be done anywhere". It is often associated with its Summer Festival, where its sumptuous productions present high art for high prices to a discerning clientele. Yet it also has an annual Tour—which in 2018 celebrated its 50th year—to five or six English cities, attracting an audience of over 40,000. It films productions for the cinema, streams live performances where it has attracted audiences of 100,000 and every three years it presents a large community opera. It has a year-round educational component, with digital resources available for children to explore how composers, performers, directors and designers all come together in the great operas. In 2016, the education programme engaged 40,000 people. It also stages a comparatively high number of UK premieres and rarely performed productions; operas state-funded companies find difficult to justify. The Festival receives no government funding. The Tour, with a budget of around £4 million, receives £1.6 million from the government's Arts Council.

Glyndebourne was founded by the current executive chairman's, Gus Christie's, grandfather, who personally funded its early years. Since the 1950s it has relied on philanthropy, and in the early days of arts sponsorship, when things were very hand-to-mouth, it received funding from cigarette companies, such as the Peter Stuyvesant Foundation and pharmaceutical firms. A membership model was created for funding performances in the 1950s. There are currently 9000 Festival Members and 5000 Associate Members, who between them purchase around three-quarters of all tickets. In 2016, the Festival sold 99% of all tickets and the Tour, 83%.

Around 30% of Glyndebourne's budget derives from membership subscriptions and fundraising through sponsorship. Almost all sponsorship comes from private donors, who give at various levels. This ranges from £300,000+ for a new production (covering around a third of the cost of a production), which can be shared, or syndicated between a group of individuals who all contribute £20,000+. Around half of new productions are funded by individuals and half are syndicated. The motivations for individual sponsorship include celebrating important birthdays and anniversaries. Gus Christie says the company has a pool of about 90 people, whom he describes as philanthropic heroes, providing £10,000-plus a year. This group is recognized at the Old Green Room Society, which allows access to pre-performance hospitality and to rehearsals.

An article on philanthropy in Glyndebourne's festival programme reveals the diverse artistic preferences of sponsors. One says he and his wife like to support the "blockbusters", such as Mozart and Verdi, because they bring money into the box office. Another says he and his wife like to support work that is rarely performed, new interpretations or new work. Both are attracted by the lack of public funding, which they say has too many strings attached. As well as funding wider audiences for its art, philanthropy allows the company to take risks and innovate.

A core concern for all sponsors is to have "impact", and one major element of this includes interest in attracting younger audiences to the opera and supporting young artists. One of the major innovations introduced by Glyndebourne is the New Generation Programme, started in 2009, aimed at artistic and audience development. The Programme was launched by the Associate Members' fee of £500, plus an individual gift of £1 million, and has received around £10 million in direct funding towards a portfolio of programmes to achieve these objectives.

As part of its support for young people, the Festival offers up to 2000 top price tickets for £30 for people under 30, through investment from the New Generation Programme. The Glyndebourne Opera Cup is an international competition for opera singers designed to discover and spotlight the best young singers from around the world. It offers a top prize of £15,000 and a platform for launching an international opera career. Glyndebourne has a Youth Opera, chorus development programme, and a debut artist and Supporting Composer Programme, aiming to further musicians' careers. One donor speaks of his pride in supporting up and coming artists who go on to become major stars. He also refers to the benefits of being a major sponsor that include getting to know the singers, conductors and directors, seeing the early stage designs, and generally being involved in the production. Another refers to the pleasure in seeing glowing reviews for performances he has supported.

The company works to understand the requirements and preferences of the membership, with several commissioned research projects into their concerns. Disquiet amongst the members at sponsorship received from a controversial daily newspaper led to its discontinuation. Glyndebourne carefully assesses major donations from individuals, with due diligence conducted through the company's eminent and very well-connected Board. Maintenance of the company's ethical reputation is said to be critical at all times. The company's artistic vision is also fiercely protected, with control never ceded to members and sponsors.

Support from corporations has changed over time. Companies find it more difficult to sponsor performances than in the past. Even when they support performances by buying blocks of 120 tickets for £60,000, they sometimes struggle to find people with the time to attend. Glyndebourne does, however, successfully offer corporate events for companies such as Christian Dior, has an exclusive sponsorship arrangement with the English sparkling winemaker, Nyetimber, and broadcasts operas through the website of the national newspaper, the *Daily Telegraph*. Some co-productions are undertaken with international opera companies and orchestras to share costs, especially for very expensive performances, such as Wagner's *Meistersinger*. A Glyndebourne shop operates on-site and online to supplement income through merchandising.

As well as funding performances, donors support infrastructure, including a new opera house, costing £30 million when it opened on 28 May 1994. Donations have funded the construction of a major new Production Hub, launched in 2019, bringing together previously dispersed staff working in technical production—carpentry, props, costumes and wigs— along with new rehearsal space. Located in an area of outstanding beauty, and built around a lovely house with elements going back to the fifteenth century, there has been a recent addition of large electricity-generating windmill. Over 90% of the site's electricity is produced through this renewable energy source.

A team of around a dozen work in Glyndebourne's development department, split into Fundraising and Membership. There are specialists, for example, overseeing relationships with Foundations and the Arts Council, and Events. A lifetime pathway approach is being developed for sponsors, beginning with stimulating the participation of young people, attracting support from those people as they get older (and wealthier), and encouraging legacy donations in wills. The latter has 150 contributors to the John Christie Legacy, and its guaranteed funding supported the construction of the Production Hub.

The economic contribution of arts institutions is rarely assessed. Glyndebourne is one of the largest businesses in the local area, with an annual turnover of around £28 million. It employs around 150 full-time staff and by including visiting artists and seasonal staff provides employment for around 1500. In 2013, it and the local Council commissioned research into Glyndebourne's impact on the East Sussex economy. It revealed that Glyndebourne's gross economic impact totalled £16 million every year. This translated into a Gross Value Added impact of £10.8 million; the equivalent of supporting 682 permanent jobs. Support for the Arts contributes significantly to the economy and jobs.

Challenges remain, such as scaling up the youth programme. Scenarios are explored, considering the impact of potential significant changes in the funding model, preparing for future shocks. New ways of funding are continually being explored, such as sponsoring a conductor, a role, or a debut singer. A successful series called "Behind the Curtain" has been launched, with analysis and explanations of the staging of particular operas and their histories. Audio-visual recordings are made of some Festival productions and distributed for sale. All new developments have to be consistent with a brand for what one sponsor calls a national institution, one where in all aspects of what it does: in the music, costumes and staging, in the whole experience of visiting, there is an unrelenting focus on excellence.

Glyndebourne is a values-driven organization, values which have proven attractive to many donors. It is innovative in its funding model, in its artistic programme, and in its community reach and environmental concerns. Its concern for sustainability extends into the maintenance and development of the art form of opera itself. Its philanthropic supporters enthusiastically embrace the encouragement of future generations of artists and their admirers.

Grange Park Opera, 60 miles from Glyndebourne, has a more recent history, but similar ambitions. It has built a new auditorium, and this and its programme is funded by an extraordinary array of imaginative sponsorships: from a Circle of Virtuous Enterprise, to the opportunity of sponsoring "an arm, a leg, a cowgirl or an assassin". It also receives no government funding. Its sister company, Pimlico Opera, founded and headed by the same impresario, Wasfi Kani, puts on operas in prisons. Since 1990 it has worked with more than 1000 prisoners, has employed ex-prisoners and taken 55,000 members of the public into prison to hear the staging of operas from Carmen to West Side Story. Prisoners are asked in their cells whether they like acting and performing; numbers volunteer and following some rehearsals a creative team chooses the cast. Five full weeks of rehearsal follow. Dress rehearsals take place in the prison gym, transformed into a theatre with lighting, seating and an orchestra. There are public performances and further stagings for other prisoners and prison staff. The outcomes of these performances demonstrate and affirm the talent and creativity of prisoners, aiding their rehabilitation.

OTHER CAUSES

Philanthropic giving extends well beyond science and the arts to a very wide range of social, cultural and environmental concerns. The USA's national parks, for example, have depended on wealthy individuals and foundations giving many categories of support, from the gift of land to museums. Rockefeller, for example, made numerous generous donations in the 1920s to Yosemite and Yellowstone parks, amongst others. It was private philanthropy that led to the creation of the National Park Service in 1916.

The humanitarian innovation ecosystem

Philanthropy has long supported humanitarian causes—defined as concerns for human welfare and happiness and the alleviation of suffering. In 2016, the Global Humanitarian Summit placed innovation on the humanitarian agenda, and by 2019 it was estimated that there were more than 800 research and innovation units, labs and other initiatives in the United Nations and amongst NGOs.[11] ELRHA, a global charity that uses research and innovation to find solutions to complex humanitarian problems has published an online guide to help individuals and organizations navigate humanitarian innovation.[12]

Research conducted at the Centre for Research in Innovation Management (CENTRIM), at the University of Brighton has analysed the humanitarian innovation ecosystem (Ramalingam et al. 2015). The research conducted an extensive literature review, a programme of expert interviews and five detailed case studies looking at cash and food, water and sanitation, shelter, emergency disease responses and financing through an innovation ecosystem lens. It explored donors, governmental organizations and NGOs and beneficiaries.

The research found that the humanitarian innovation ecosystem is complex, and comprised of numerous organizations, groups and individuals. It found that while there was growing recognition of the importance of innovation amongst some in the sector, there were numerous challenges, including:

• Continuing ignorance or scepticism of the contribution of innovation;
• Insularity and "not-invented-here syndrome";
• Limited or poorly allocated resources for innovation;
• Lack of skills and competencies needed for innovation;
• Little understanding of the innovation process.
    The studies suggested that improving the ecosystem requires:

- A clear sense of overall strategic vision by participants around which to focus;
- Sufficient supply of key resources—especially finance and human resources—and clear routes to enable these to flow into the system;
- High levels of openness on the knowledge supply side, with networks feeding in and recombining ideas from different sources;
- Well-articulated sense of user needs delivered by high levels of user consultation, involvement and co-creation;
- Capacity for ambidextrous working to enable both incremental and radical innovation.

Humanitarian innovation, as in the case of "social innovation", faces similar innovation management challenges to those found in the private sector (see Dodgson et al. 2014), and could benefit from the application of good practices.

Philanthropy played a central role in the Northern Ireland peace process. Atlantic Philanthropies, and its benefactor, Chuck Feeney, dedicated significant resources, estimated to be $1 billion, and effort towards bringing peace to the religious conflict in Northern Ireland (Knox and Quirk 2016). During the 1990s he made substantial donations to Northern Irish universities, but his giving was significantly more active, and indeed, controversial. He invested where governments feared to tread. He is reported to have donated to both political parties in the sectarian divide, in a programme to encourage highly politicized ex-prisoners to engage in community development, and in a community restorative justice project aimed at preventing the beatings and shooting of young people by paramilitaries. The focus was strongly on human rights in the belief that a robust, diverse and independent civic society holds the government accountable to deliver on its human rights and equality obligations. The 1998 Good Friday Agreement, the Northern Ireland peace accord, resulted from the combination of many factors, but many acknowledge the contribution of Feeney, both through his Foundation and his activities behind the scenes. The President of Sinn Féin, one of the main protagonists, said Feeney had accelerated the peace process and saved scores of lives.

Broad-based impact: the case of Atlantic Philanthropies[13]
By 2012, the CEO of Atlantic Philanthropies' claimed it had:
Promoted reconciliation and peace in Northern Ireland and South Africa.
Transformed key university infrastructure and research capacity in the Republic of Ireland, Northern Ireland, South Africa, Vietnam and the United States.
Successfully campaigned to abolish the juvenile death penalty in the United States and to abolish the death penalty in five states, with further significant prospects underway.
Advanced same-sex civil partnerships in the Republic of Ireland and gay marriage in South Africa.
Transformed major health care facilities and enhanced health care system practices to measurably improve and save lives in Vietnam. Encouraged the use of motorcycle helmets, saving numerous Vietnamese lives.
Strengthened world-class biomedical research in Australia.
Changed the perception of HIV/AIDS and secured access to antiretrovirals for millions of people in South Africa.
Recovered billions of dollars in unclaimed government benefits for over 2 million older adults in the United States and Northern Ireland.
Strengthened civil society organizations and philanthropy in Bermuda.
Fought to secure health care for children in the United States.
Transformed end-of-life care in the Republic of Ireland.

As well as contributing centrally to the maintenance of so many important social institutions, philanthropy can also be seen to promote innovation within them. This extends beyond more adventurous research and artistic performance, and can encourage difficult organizational changes on a small scale and innovative bold political transformations of international significance.

NOTES

1. "IBM v Carnegie Corporation: The Centenarians Square Up", *The Economist*, June 9, 2011.
2. World Health Organization, *Visual Impairment and Blindness*, http://www.who.int/mediacentre/factsheets/fs282/en/.
3. https://www.ellisonfoundation.org/.
4. https://alleninstitute.org/.
5. William Broad, "Billionaires with Big Ideas Are Privatizing American Science", *New York Times*, March 16, 2014.

6. http://philanthropy.coutts.com.
7. http://www.bloomberg.com/news/2014-09-08/harvard-gets-record-350-million-gift-for-public-health.html.
8. https://www.hsph.harvard.edu/news/features/commencement-2012-remarks-chan/.
9. Gerald Chan, "2017 Yale Innovation Summit", http://ocr.yale.edu/news/gerald-chan-keynote-university-and-biotechnology.
10. https://www.stradivarisociety.com/; http://www.amatifoundation.org/; https://benslowmusic-ils.org/.
11. http://www.thenewhumanitarian.org/analysis/2019/03/20/humanitarian-innovation-faces-rethink-innovators-take-stock.
12. https://higuide.elrha.org/.
13. See e.g. C. Oechsli (2012). *Thirty Years of Giving While Living: Our Final Chapter*. New York: Atlantic Philanthropies, http://www.atlanticphilanthropies.org/.

REFERENCES

Acs, Z. (2013). *Why Philanthropy Matters*. Princeton, NJ: Princeton University Press.
Anheier, H., & Leat, D. (2006). *Creative Philanthropy: Towards a New Philanthropy for the 21st Century*. London and New York: Routledge.
Beveridge, W. (1942). *Social Insurance and Allied Services*. London: HMSO.
Blair, K. (2005). Philanthropy for Women's Art in America, Past and Present. In A. Walton (Ed.), *Women and Philanthropy in Education*. Bloomington: Indiana University Press.
Callahan, D. (2017). *The Givers: Wealth, Power, and Philanthropy in a New Gilded Age*. New York: Knopf.
Chen, J. (2017). *Clearly*. London: Biteback Books.
Crocker, R. (2005). "Nothing More for Men's Colleges": The Educational Philanthropy of Mrs. Russell Sage. In A. Walton (Ed.), *Women and Philanthropy in Education*. Bloomington: Indiana University Press.
Dodgson, M. (2017). Innovation in Firms. *Oxford Review of Economic Policy, 33*(1), 85–100.
Dodgson, M., Gann, D., & Phillips, N. (Eds.). (2014). *The Oxford Handbook of Innovation Management*. Oxford: Oxford University Press.
Dodgson, M., & Staggs, J. (2012). Government Policy, University Strategy and the Academic Entrepreneur: The Case of Queensland's Smart State Institutes. *Cambridge Journal of Economics, 36*(2), 567–586.
Knox, C., & Quirk, P. (2016). *Public Policy, Philanthropy and Peacebuilding in Northern Ireland*. London: Palgrave Macmillan.

McGoey, L. (2015). *No Such Thing as a Free Gift.* London: Verso.

Mulgan, G., Tucker, S., Ali, R., & Sanders, B. (2007). *Social Innovation: What It Is, Why It Matters and How It Can Be Accelerated.* Oxford: Young Foundation/Said Business School.

Murray, F. (2012). *Evaluating the Role of Science Philanthropy in American Research Universities* (NBER Working Paper No. 18146).

Nielson, W. (2002). *Golden Donors.* New Brunswick, NJ: Transaction Publishers.

O'Clery, C. (2007). *The Billionaire Who Wasn't: How Chuck Feeney Secretly Made and Gave Away a Fortune.* New York: Public Affairs.

Ostrower, F. (1997). *Why the Wealthy Give: The Culture of Elite Philanthropy.* Princeton, NJ: Princeton University Press.

Ramalingam, B., Rush, H., Bessant, J., Marshall, N., Gray, B., Hoffman, K., et al. (2015). *Strengthening the Humanitarian Innovation Ecosystem.* Humanitarian Innovation Ecosystem Research Project Final Report, Brighton University.

Rittel, H., & Webber, M. (1973). Dilemmas in a General Theory of Planning. *Policy Sciences, 4*(2), 155–169.

Schneider, W. (2002). *Rockefeller Philanthropy and Modern Biomedicine: International Initiatives from World War I to the Cold War.* Bloomington, IN: Indiana University Press.

Seim, D. (2013). *Rockefeller Philanthropy and Modern Social Science.* London: Pickering & Chatto Publishers.

Upchurch, A. (2016). Philanthropists and Policy Advisors. In *The Origins of the Arts Council Movement.* New Directions in Cultural Policy Research. London: Palgrave Macmillan.

Wolf Ditkoff, S., & Grindle, A. (2017, September–October). Audacious Philanthropy. *Harvard Business Review*, pp. 110–118.

Zinsmeister, K. (2016). How Philanthropy Fuels American Success. In *The Almanac of American Philanthropy.* Washington, DC: Philanthropy Roundtable.

CHAPTER 4

The Governance of Philanthropy

Abstract This chapter analyses the governance of philanthropy: how philanthropic giving is managed and structured. It describes the difficulties in giving effectively and efficiently. The central role of, and challenges faced by, foundations are outlined. A case study of philanthropy improving children's numeracy in Africa is provided. Corporate philanthropy is discussed. The issues related to attracting and using philanthropy are traversed and there is explanation on how campaigns are constructed, and cautions raised about over-dependence.

Keywords Governance of philanthropy · Management of philanthropy · Importance and challenges of foundations · Corporate philanthropy · Philanthropic campaigns

Giving It Away

There is an old adage about money, that "you can't take it with you", to which billionaires, such as Michael Bloomberg, add "you can't spend it". Simply, the resources of the super-rich can grow quicker than they can disperse them. *Forbes* listed over 2000 billionaires in its 2017 list, with a total worth of $7.7 trillion. If, hypothetically, they were to sign the Giving Pledge, agreeing to give half their wealth away and that amount were to be invested and produce a 5% return, then that amounts to over $150 billion in interest earned each year. That is more than the GDP of all but 14 countries in the world. Capgemini in its World Wealth Report shows that some 150,000 people around the world have a net worth in excess of $30 million.[1]

The difficulties of giving money away have been commented upon since Aristotle. Andrew Carnegie noted that giving money intelligently is harder than earning it. John D. Rockefeller Snr's 1909 book had a chapter entitled "The Difficult Art of Giving", and said the ever-widening field of philanthropic endeavour had led him almost to a nervous breakdown. He also said what people most seek cannot be bought with money. It does not necessarily follow that those best at making money are the best at giving it away. Olivia Sage made it her mission in the early twentieth century to improve higher educational opportunities for women (Crocker 2005), but was beset with broken promises from universities, such as New York University, to which she had donated. As a result of the influence of her advisors and perhaps distracted by the prestige of the institutions she supported—including Yale, Harvard, Princeton and Cornell—she donated heavily to universities that only accepted men.

In addition to the rather vital question of how much they give, philanthropists need to choose what to support and the best methods to do so. Some, according to Skocpol (2016): "engage focus on policy change, being actively involved in every stage of the policy process: formulating and amplifying ideas, creating policy networks with common goals, and pushing coordinated reform agendas".

To encourage the innovation and change they seek, the question is how is the giving by philanthropists best governed; that is, what rules, relationships, systems and processes most effectively disperse their funds?

The great philanthropists of the past, the Rockefellers and Carnegies, tended to make their money first, then give it away. Andrew Carnegie's 1889 book, *The Gospel of Wealth*, argued the moral obligation of the wealthy to give back most of their money before they died. This model might also be used to describe Bill Gates's philanthropy, and he is often compared to Carnegie. Some philanthropists manage to give their money away before they die, such as Eastman and Milton Hershey. Chuck Feeney, of Atlantic Philanthropies, wants his funds dispersed before he dies: the foundation completed its grant-making in 2016, and will be wound up completely in 2020. His approach is "giving while living". This is also the case with some younger technology philanthropists, such as Facebook's Chan and Zuckerberg and Dustin Moskovitz, who aim to give their money away while they are young. Others such as Gordon Moore and Bill Hewlett give their money away when they retire. Ostrower's (1997) study of the wealthy elite of New York, found that having led active professional lives, philanthropy provides an arena where philanthropists can direct their energy and expertise following retirement. Some wish to create enduring foundations that continue for a period after their death. Many founders of foundations stipulate that funds have to be spent within 25 years or a generation after their death. Bill and Melinda Gates plan their foundation's demise 20 years after the death of the longest-lived. Others, such as Ford, Rockefeller, Wellcome and Wolfson establish enduring foundations.

This sometimes raises issues of intergenerational philanthropy. Some children of philanthropists, such as the three children of Warren Buffet, become influential philanthropists themselves; others pursue other interests. The Sainsbury family is one of the largest benefactors to philanthropy and charity in the UK. Its three generations of philanthropists pursue their particular interests within 17 independent grant-making trusts, which have an operating office, the Sainsbury Family Charitable Trusts, providing economies of scale in the management of the various trusts. Family considerations can become fraught as philanthropists decide how much they should leave their children and how much they should give away. The Koch family has been riven with familial legal disputes. Warren Buffet's approach to this is to leave his children "enough money so that they would feel they could do anything, but not so much that they could do nothing".

Should philanthropists support foundations that are self-perpetuating or self-exhausting? Some argue that long-lived foundations can fail to meet the objectives of their founders. The Pew Freedom Trust and the Ford Foundation, for example, are believed to have funded projects that would have outraged the extreme political sentiments of their creators. Numbers of studies exist of the subversion of donor intent by professionals and academic advisers. Sir Peter Moores, who gave over £200 million to the arts in the UK, wound his foundation up 50 years after he started it. He said he would want someone good to run the foundation after his death, and as they would be good they would have their own ideas, which might not be his: hence his decision to spend it all. As the case of the Wellcome Trust shows, however, it is possible to remain faithful to the founder's intent.

Continuity and evolution of foundation objectives: the Wellcome Trust[2]

The Wellcome Trust is the largest philanthropic organization in the UK, with a portfolio of over £20 billion, focussing on the biosciences. It was originally created from the wealth of Sir Henry Wellcome (1853–1936), a pioneer in pharmaceutical research and the pharmaceutical industry. Sir Henry's 1932 will established two funds, a Research Museum and Library Fund and a Research Fund. The former was to study the sciences allied to medicine, or their history, the latter was to support the advancement of research work. The will stipulated that the nature and objects of research should be: "medicine surgery chemistry physiology bacteriology therapeutics materia medica pharmacy and allied subject (sic)" and noted Sir Henry's especial concern for insects and pests that afflict humans, animals and plants in tropical regions.

The will included two stipulations about the funds that proved to be prescient and wise. The first was despite Sir Henry's suggestions, research could be conducted on: "any subject or subjects which have or may at any time develop importance for scientific research that may conduce to the improvement of the physical conditions of mankind...". The second was his concern to "ensure that the results of the researches supported by the Fund will be made available by full and unrestricted publication, for the benefit of mankind".

The objects of the Wellcome Trust today are:

1. to protect, preserve and advance all or any aspects of the health and welfare of humankind and to advance and promote knowledge and education by engaging in, encouraging and supporting:

    (a) research into any of the biosciences; and
    (b) the discovery, invention, improvement, development and application of treatments, cures, diagnostics and other medicinal agents, methods and processes that may in any way relieve, illness, disease, disability or disorders of whatever nature in human beings or animals or plant life; and

2. to advance and promote knowledge and education by engaging in, encouraging and supporting:

    (a) research into the history of any of the biosciences; and
    (b) the study and understanding of any of the biosciences or the history of any of the biosciences.

The language has modernized, but it is clear the intent remains the same. Wellcome also has an open access policy of unrestricted access to the published output of its research. Authors of research papers, monographs and book chapters receiving Wellcome funding are expected to maximize the opportunities to make their results freely available. Wellcome contributed substantially to the international Human Genome Project, ensuring that sequence data was published freely and quickly. Wellcome has a fund to pay for access fees from publishers. Sir Henry's wishes are still being respected.

As highlighted by Callahan (2017), there are differences amongst new generation philanthropists between those with a technology and finance background. Technology entrepreneurs are good at identifying opportunities and taking risks, and many bring these capacities to their philanthropy. They are also ambitious, impatient and occasionally brash and look for major results from their donations. Disruption in their world is something sought and beneficial. As with innovation in general, failure is common, and to be expected. Collaboration is normal and there is an emphasis on shared learning (Dodgson et al. 2014). Sean Parker of Napster and Facebook, describes this approach as "hacker philanthropy", and he is applying it in the $250 million Parker Institute for Cancer Immunotherapy he has created to reshape the field of cancer immunology. His objective is to dramatically speed up the development of new drugs. Hacker philanthropy, according Parker, has very different characteristics than the older, well-established foundations.[3] It provides an alternative to the incremental and conservative approach of most foundations whose activities he contends are shaped by the concern for self-preservation. Like many new generation philanthropists, there is little recognition of the scientific and business-like approach to giving pursued by the early foundations, such as Carnegie and Rockefeller.

Philanthropists from a finance background, from the world of hedge funds and derivatives, have a different view. Their decisions are data-driven and their perspectives are based on market efficiency and hyper-competition where the slightest edge of insight or information provides great returns. Cooperation and sharing is not part of their world-view, and is often illegal in the businesses they lead. Many philanthropists who have thrived on Wall Street are more traditional in their giving, supporting arts institutions and Ivy League universities. They are more inured to the world of policymaking and the opaque but very real power of the privileged elite than the society neophyte entrepreneurs of Silicon Valley. Many who have worked in the technology industry or in risk-taking finance appreciate a portfolio approach, commonly found in innovation strategies, whereby a proportion of investments are high risk/high return. Many of these investments will fail, but the extraordinary returns of a small proportion of them more than compensates. This is characteristic of so-called venture philanthropy. On the matter of tolerance of risk, it is notable that private family philanthropists are accountable primarily, and often exclusively, to the family. Risks are theirs to bear, not trustees or shareholders, and this can lead to adventurous investments.

Many successful people are not short-changed in the ego department, and hubris and enthusiastic self-advancement is not unknown amongst philanthropists (Giridharadas 2018). This is consequential when it prevents proper appreciation of the complexity of many problems attempting to be addressed, and when the solutions to these problems are shaped by the, often limited, experiences of the entrepreneur. If I solved a technological problem this way, why can't I solve a social problem in the same manner? The sociologist Paul Schervish (2003) explains the concept of "hyperagency" when it comes to philanthropists, and particularly donors from high-tech industries, which he defines as "the array of dispositions and capacities that enable individuals to relatively singlehandedly produce the social outcomes they desire, as well as the conditions within which they and others exercise their agency". Such ambition is also captured in an article in *Harvard Business Review* by Susan Wolf Ditkoff and Abe Grindle (2017):

> Many of today's emerging large-scale philanthropists aspire to similarly audacious successes. They don't want to fund homeless shelters and food pantries; they want to end homelessness and hunger. Steady, linear progress isn't enough; they demand disruptive, catalytic, systemic change—and in short order. Even as society grapples with important questions about today's concentrations of wealth, many of the largest philanthropists feel the weight of responsibility that comes with their privilege. And the scale of their ambition, along with the wealth they are willing to give back to society, is breathtaking.

There are many guides written on how to give more effectively, but there are distinctive approaches. Michael Bloomberg is reputed to be led by data, informing how his money can be put to most use. Howard Buffett, in contrast, argues it is best to forget all the standard metrics of success that foundations obsess over, and he relies on intuition and judgement. Generally, however, information needs to be made available to ensure decisions are made wisely, and whether grants and donations are producing the expected returns. But this has to be undertaken in circumstances where major changes result from many interdependent forces, and the complexity of problems makes causality of particular interventions difficult to establish. As with all significant endeavours, fortunate timing and luck always have roles to play.

The best place to start is with the problem philanthropists wish to address. Thomas Tierney and Joel Fleishman (2012) argue that philanthropists often fail to meet their objectives because they are not clear enough about their aims and coherent enough in explaining what those aims are. Giving money away is easy, they say, but giving it away smartly so it gets results that continue to improve is hard. Philanthropists face four traps: "fuzzy-headedness", of not knowing precise objectives; flying solo, not appreciating how difficult it is to accomplish change by yourself; underestimating and underinvesting and failing to invest in general operating support. They suggest philanthropists should address six questions:

Six key questions for philanthropists
What are my values and beliefs?
What is "success" and how can it be achieved?
What am I accountable for?
What will it take to get the job done?
How do I work with grantees?
Am I getting better?

The study of 15 profound philanthropic interventions cited in Wolf Ditkoff and Grindle (2017) identified five elements explaining their success:

Build a shared understanding of the problem and its ecosystem. They found the leaders of these interventions appreciated and carefully framed the issues they sought to address. They knew who was affected and what forces perpetuated problems. They had deep appreciation of the root causes of problems and their entrenched racial, cultural and economic dynamics, understanding who benefited from, and would fight to preserve, the status quo; and built evidence bases that propelled action.

Set "winnable milestones" and hone a compelling message. They found their leaders kept people motivated and engaged by identifying concrete, measurable goals, what they call "winnable milestones", and pairing them with emotionally compelling messages or calls to action.

Design approaches that will work at massive scale. They found success depends on impact at scale, and there are many ways of achieving this, but they often first require innovation and experimentation.

Drive (rather than assume) demand. The successful cases invested in solutions that users and partners actually wanted. Their leaders funded robust sales and marketing efforts to support ambitious goals. They worked with governments to create new regulations. And they provided easy access to the solutions to the problems they addressed by ensuring strong distribution networks.

Embrace course corrections. The study found funders need to support their grantees' capacity to continuously improve. Social impact organizations need to experiment, measure, and adapt as circumstances change over time, and philanthropists need to invest deeply in creating the space and infrastructure for grantees to learn, adjust, and at times fail. Entrepreneurs recognize this as pivoting.

Although this study points to the importance of continuity of giving, occasionally over many decades, there may be circumstances where there are benefits to benefactions having shorter durations. One of philanthropy's greatest contributions can lie in its ability to take a catalytic role in helping raise a problem, and then identify how to address it. In such situations, having successfully "pump primed", philanthropic support can be withdrawn, confident that the problem has been resolved or other actors, including those who were the target of the benefaction, have the capacity to address it themselves.

Much can be learned on governance from the approaches of leading philanthropists. Michael Bloomberg, founder of the eponymous financial services and media companies and former mayor of New York, is one of the most generous and successful philanthropists.[4] In 2016, he donated over $600 million to more than 1000 organizations in the arts, education, the environment, government innovation, and public health. Over his lifetime, he has given over $5 billion. The approach to his philanthropy is to: focus on cities to drive progress, look for unmet needs that can be addressed with proven solutions, rely on data and continually measure progress, lead from the front and do not hesitate to address controversial issues, utilize advocacy and lobbying, identify and engage strong partners and remain flexible to invest boldly and quickly in order to maximize impact. The funder of major projects addressing issues from fighting the obesity epidemic to preventing drowning, he has also been involved in very small-scale initiatives, such as when with Al Gore he painted a roof white in Queens, New York. Mocked for doing it, the white roofs reflected rather than absorbed heat, immediately reduced electricity bills and has since been replicated throughout the borough.[5]

Ted Turner, of CNN fame, another leading American philanthropist, made the bold decision in 1997 to give $1 billion to the United Nations. Recognizing the challenges facing the organization, especially its notorious bureaucracy, but also appreciating its capacities, Turner's contribution helped create the United Nations Foundation, which attracted further donations and has made a number of beneficial interventions, in, for example, the provision of tens of thousands of mosquito nets.

One area of especial controversy is in charter schools that operate independently from government control. Many high-profile philanthropists have been attracted to support these initiatives in the face of deteriorating standards and performance of state schools. Yet, charter schools have stirred considerable opposition, especially from teaching unions and some local authorities and research and advocacy groups. Concerns are raised about the lack of evidence of outcomes, and the creation of dual systems of educational opportunity and quality. There are also accusations in some instances of administrative malpractice and profiteering. Some initiatives, such as the $100 million Mark Zuckerberg invested in Newark, New York, are considered to have failed because the school reforms lacked local support. Undeterred, the Chan Zuckerberg Foundation subsequently invested $120 million in schools in San Francisco, vowing to engage fully with the community. There are deep and persistent problems with the public educational system in the USA, and elsewhere, that will continue to attract the attention of philanthropists, inspired to produce much-needed improvements. Yet the field is so complex, and political opinions on the best paths for the future are so polarized, that philanthropic engagement is likely to remain difficult and challenging. It is notable how Mark Zuckerberg and Priscilla Chan refer to the importance of learning from their experiences and attempting to become better givers. A key to effective governance is effective reflection and learning.

Concern for the environment attracts substantial donations from organizations such as Tom Steyer's NextGen America, and ClimateWorks Foundation, but overall this issue receives a relatively small proportion of philanthropic giving at around 1–2% of the total. While the amount given is increasing, many in the field question the level of contributions given the significance of the problem. Along with the sheer scale of the environmental issues to be confronted, there is a challenge, it is felt, in the lack of immediacy in the problem compared to other issues, such as alleviating poverty. The solution, it is felt, lies with increasing cooperation and coordination between givers, and greater focus on the immediate outcomes of climate change, such as famine and increased numbers of refugees.

Wendy Schmidt and Eric Schmidt, the ex-chairman of Google, created a philanthropic foundation in 2006 with a strong focus on environmental issues, and especial concern for the health of the oceans. In 2009, they launched the Schmidt Ocean Institute, with its own research vessel. They stipulated that ocean researchers can use the ship provided they make their data freely available within two months of their research trip. Wendy Schmidt has increasingly focussed her attention on the oceans, sponsoring competitions to address their pollution. In 2010, following the Deep Horizon disaster, $1.4 was offered to find new ways of dealing with oil spills. In 2015 $2 million was offered to develop sensors to accurately measure ocean acidity.

Wendy Schmidt says she sees her role of her ocean-related philanthropy as promoting proper management and increasing public awareness.[6] The foundation's research vessel has a berth for a resident artist to communicate about the ocean and its challenges. She believes that although there are massive challenges, technological solutions are possible, and unleashing those technologies is one of the thrills of philanthropy.

FOUNDATIONS

Foundations offer grants to support particular causes and operate their own projects to address distinct problems. Some focus on one of these activities, some do both. A number of foundations have enormous budgets and staff levels and concomitantly significant influence. The Gates' Foundation, for example, has an endowment of over $50 billion, employs 1500, and in 2017 gave over $4 billion in grants. Its giving exceeds that of the nine other largest foundations combined. Despite its extraordinary generosity, McGoey (2015) takes a critical view of the influence of the Gates' Foundation, citing, for example, how it provides 10% of the World

Health Organization's overall budget, donating more than any government. This, she argues, gives the Foundation disproportionate influence over global health policy issues.

Many scholars of philanthropy credit the influential and successful Baltimore investor George Peabody for the invention of American philanthropy. And many suggest, given its considerable achievements, that the exemplar model of philanthropic foundation is the Rockefeller Foundation. The first large American foundations, such as Rockefeller and Carnegie, were dedicated to the professionalization of giving. Their founders had built their companies on scientific principles of organization and efficiency and were determined to use the same approach in their foundations. The Rockefellers have been likened to the House of Medici in fifteenth- and sixteenth-century Florence, for the impact they have had (Loebl 2010). As well as eventually developing a vaccine for Yellow Fever, Rockefeller funds, according to Acs (2013), supported the eradication of hookworm in the American South; the development of penicillin; the establishment of public-health schools (today's undisputed leaders in their fields) all over the world; the establishment of medical facilities in all parts of the globe; the creation and funding of great research centres such as the University of Chicago, the Brookings Institution, Rockefeller University, and the National Bureau of Economic Research; the control of malaria in Brazil; the founding of the research centres that accomplished the green revolution in Asia and more.

Some donors use intermediaries who bundle together a number of contributors to have a larger fund to donate. The largest of these donor-advised funds is Fidelity, which works with over 100,000 donors and is the second largest grant-making body after the Gates' Foundation. Donors can choose which charities to give to, and their donations are immediately tax deductible. Mayer (2016) criticizes these structures as they break the direct and hence transparent link between donors and causes, and they remove the engagement element in our definition of philanthropy.

Foundations can coordinate their efforts, for example in the 10-year collaboration between the Carnegie, Ford, Hewlett, Krege, MacArthur, Mellon and Rockefeller Foundations working together until 2010 to assist the development of African Higher Education. Each contributed in its own way, with common efforts in, for example, reducing broadband costs in universities. Fabrice Jaumont (2016) in a book on this subject argues it is difficult to assess the impact of private US foundations on the development of African higher education, but says their influence has never been neutral, and have offered direction and authority towards infusing policy with a Western perspective.

Foundation CEOs can be immensely influential, but they face continual challenges in investing for the long-term versus dealing with immediate demands and contributing to well-known versus emerging problems. Fay Twersky (2014) interviewed 45 past or present foundation CEOs whose jobs she describes as "artful juggling". She says they must tend to their board of directors, manage their organization internally, and ensure their foundation's efforts are impactful. Twersky says by their own reckoning, few CEOs are equally successful in all three areas.

Edwin Rogers Embree was one of the most influential foundation leaders, having been second in charge of the Rockefeller Foundation, then President of the Julius Rosenwald Fund, in the 1930s and 40s. Well-travelled and author of numerous books and articles, Embree was an expert on race relations, and engaged in a career of over 30 years with school reform, civil rights, scientific research, the arts, state and national politics, higher education, world affairs. According to his biographer, Alfred Perkins,

> His career was marked by remarkable imagination and uncommon boldness, by an eagerness to push organized giving in new directions and toward greater effectiveness.... He was often in contention—with southern governors, conservative midwesterners, physicians suspicious of the neighborhood clinics he promoted.... (Perkins 2011)

His leadership skills must have been fully tested when, during the market collapse of the Great Depression, almost all of the assets of the Rosenwald were wiped out. Yet the Trust continued its work, especially supporting the education of Black people in the South of the USA, until all funds were depleted in 1948.

There have long been concerns over the efficiency of philanthropic organizations, with poor governance and decision-making. Prochaska (1990) refers to the concern for the way in eighteenth- and nineteenth-century Britain pressure was put on people who could not afford it to give money to those that did not deserve it.

The role of the Board of Trustees of foundations is crucial. Governance mechanisms—affecting strategies on the one hand and funding decisions and accountability on the other—can be less stringent than for private companies, despite in some cases very large amounts of money being

involved. Reich (2013) points to the way foundations have certain obligations of procedural accountability, such that in the USA, a "payout" rule
mandates that foundations disburse at least five percent of their assets
every year. He also points out that the costs of running a foundation
count toward this payout. Foundations are also required to file an annual
tax form with some basic data about trustees, employees and their salaries
and assets. Despite this, he contends that foundations can, and frequently
do, act secretly. "They need not have a Web site or office, publish an
annual or quarterly report, or articulate any grant-making strategy. They
need not evaluate their grant making. If they do, they need not make
such evaluations public".

Foundations face considerable scrutiny over their operating costs. It is
not uncommon for foundation overheads to be about 15–20% of annual
budgets. Some argue these costs are immaterial as what matters is positive
outcomes, and effective use of donor money can require highly skilled and
well-trained staff, and efficient processes and information and technology
systems, which can be costly.

High-quality management is needed to ensure effective organizational
processes and decision-making, and prevent scandals of financial misuse
or staff misbehaviour that could prove devastating to reputations. Oxfam
suffered from severe reputational damage when it was discovered in 2018
that staff members sexually abused women following Haiti's devastating
hurricane in 2010. New procedures were subsequently introduced to prevent and report misconduct.

There are voices concerned about the power of foundations, that do
not have politicians' need to heed their constituents, or businesses' need
to respond to market competitors or customer demands. Reich (2013)
puts it this way:

> A democratic society is committed, at least in principle, to the equality
> of citizens. But foundations are, virtually by definition, the voice of plu-
> tocracy. The assets of a modern philanthropic foundation are set aside in
> a permanent, donor-directed, tax-advantaged private endowment and dis-
> tributed for a public purpose. These considerable private assets give it con-
> siderable public power. And with growing wealth and income inequality,
> their apparent tension with democratic principles only intensifies.

Skocpol (2016) also notes another form of potential distortion—the
feeling of many recipients of foundation grants—when she says. "The

routines that foundations follow will permeate the goals and routines of grantees – even if the net result is to cause most groups to neglect their substantive missions and focus instead on the short term, as they scramble for the next foundation grant". Such impacts can be highly significant, given the number and size of foundation grants to universities. In 2012 in the USA, for example, Johns Hopkins University received 221 grants of $10,000 or more totalling $166 million; Harvard received 325 grants totalling $91 million; and Stanford received 372 grants totalling $89 million.[7]

This points to another possible effect of philanthropy. As noted by the economist Avner Offer giving gives rise to obligation, in other words, a debt: the giver notches up an emotional and material credit, in the form of a bond on the recipient (Offer 1997).

The following case demonstrates that sometimes it is not the amount of funding that matters, but its timing and quality. It also shows that, as in the case of Chuck Feeney, in addition to good processes and procedures, personal judgements of people matter.

FROM LITTLE ACORNS...

Following the decades of apartheid, the South African education system has struggled to produce the number of numerically skilled school leavers needed to build a modern economy. There are some claims that maths education in South Africa is amongst the worst in the world.

Former investment analyst and Harvard physics graduate, Andrew Einhorn, set out to do something to improve the situation, especially amongst the most disadvantaged children living in township areas. With funding from the David and Elaine Potter Foundation he embarked on the mission: "to help young South Africans excel in mathematics by providing high-quality after-school programs and training new maths teachers".

David and Elaine Potter are originally from South Africa; David is a physicist who founded Psion software company, Elaine is a political scientist and author. The Potter Foundation supported Andrew's Master's degree with a scholarship, and he met David and Elaine for lunch once or twice each year. At one of these lunches, Elaine and he got talking about education. A few weeks later, she sent him an email with a link to Salman Khan's TED talk on online learning, and asked if he thought it could be used in South Africa. He responded that he wasn't sure, but he'd like to give it a try. She asked what he needed to do so, and as a result the first pilot got launched with £3000 in seed funding to run a three-month pilot.

To turn vision into reality, Andrew created Numeric in 2011, starting with one classroom of 17 Grade 7 (final year of primary school) learners in Cape Town, which he taught himself. It has since grown each year: from 1 to 7 classrooms, then 22, then 46 then 70 and in 2016, 97 classrooms of after-school maths, reaching over 2100 students. Numeric has grown from a staff of three to 15 full-time staff, 85 part-time coaches, and is actively involved in training teachers to teach maths. Numeric began using online learning platforms and subsequently gathered from the results of its monitoring and evaluation, that far more important than the technology was the quality of the facilitator put in the classroom. Today Numeric invests considerable energy and resources in its coach recruitment and training processes, with very positive results.

The organization has attracted further funding from the Omidyar Network, the Oppenheimer Memorial Trust, the Mapula Trust and several corporate social investment funds. Over 5000 children have completed Numeric's year-long course, in partnership with 40 primary schools across Cape Town and Johannesburg. Numeric is independently evaluated and results show that Numeric learners consistently improve by between 50 and 60% over the course of the year, almost twice as much as their peers.

Andrew considers that this philanthropy-funded model was the only way to provide high-quality learning experiences in township areas. Alternatives, such as not-for-profits, still require students to pay something so the efforts become self-sustaining, but this is not viable where there is such poverty and disadvantage.

The role of the Potter Foundation has been crucial in suggesting the idea in the first place and in providing critical feedback, encouragement and input on Numeric's first set of pilot studies. Andrew says that David's experience in business and Elaine's general acuity provided useful underpinnings in the early days. In 2018, Numeric received an investment of £280,000 from a South African impact investor, E2, towards sponsoring classrooms, building capacity in Numeric, and potential expansion into other provinces.

As well as the considerable returns that can be achieved from relatively small amounts of money, judicious investments can help leverage larger projects. Lord Dainton, a Trustee of the Wolfson Foundation in the 1980s, said that "The 'money at the margins' often has an influence in enabling good ideas to bear fruit which is far greater than its sheer monetary value would suggest".

The Wolfson Foundation is one of the UK's most important philanthropic organizations. Since its formation in 1955 it has developed a clear policy for its giving in which leveraging and partnerships are crucial. In its report to celebrate its 60th anniversary, it summarizes its policy as:

> First, it has always sought to support excellence (both existing and potential) usually by the provision of essential and enabling infrastructure. This has been based on the advice provided by expert panels and increasingly sophisticated expert review of applications. Secondly, it has continually sought to identify and nurture important areas that are under-funded. Thirdly, applicants have been encouraged to use Wolfson funds as a catalyst: as a way of levering additional support. Fourthly, and from the outset, the Foundation has sought collaboration with other expert bodies and it has established fruitful partnerships with the country's leading learned societies (notably the Royal Society and British Academy), other grant-making bodies, such as the Wellcome Trust, government departments and charities...[8]

CORPORATE PHILANTHROPY

Milton Friedman famously claimed that the social responsibility of business is to increase its profits. This view, that companies should absent themselves from any philanthropic activities, was strongly argued on two grounds by his older colleague and fellow Nobel Prize-winning economist Friedrich Hayek. First, that companies don't know anything about philanthropic causes, and would give money away inefficiently. Second, when managers make decisions about where to give money they are imposing their own preferences over the good of the company shareholders and in this sense such giving is theft. Somewhat ironically, Hayek's academic post at the University of Chicago was not funded by the university, but by businessman William Volker's charitable Trust.

One question to arise when it comes to considering the role of corporations to the public good is whether the greatest contributions lies in companies pursuing their business objectives, rather than from giving. Has Bill Gates' greatest contribution to human welfare, for example, come from his philanthropy or his software?

Corporate philanthropy is increasing. The Economist reports that in America corporate philanthropy doubled in real terms between 1990 and 2015, to $18 billion, and a study of 20 European countries showed that corporations gave about €22 billion ($26 billion) in 2013, more than foundations did.[9] Companies give to good causes directly and through specialist foundations they establish that develop expertise in giving and have a degree of independence from the company. The largest company foundations in the UK in 2016, each giving over £17 million, were BHP Billiton, Lloyds, Shell, Vodafone and Goldman Sachs. Denmark's Novo Nordisk Foundation is one of the world's largest foundations, with funds approaching $50 billion in 2018. With a history going back to 1922, the Foundation is the primary owner of Novo Nordisk, the Danish pharmaceutical company, and funds medical research and treatment.

Philanthropic giving by businesses commonly, but not always, resides within the remit of Corporate Social Responsibility (CSR). CSR is premised on the view that corporate success depends upon the way due attention is paid to the society and environment in which companies operate. CSR investments can also promote the business, so, for example, in India where CSR spending of 2% of profits is a legal requirement for large companies, a truck-maker promotes driving lessons, a consumer products company offers beauty lesson, and banks provide lessons to improve financial literacy. Furthermore, demands from employees and customers for responsible behaviour that is ethical, socially beneficial and not environmentally damaging, adds to company incentives to create CSR activities and roles.

Kurt Hoffman was the founder and first director of the Shell Foundation (1997–2008), and he developed a strategy for Shell that made business investments to achieve both social/philanthropic and investment goals. The Foundation blurred the lines between creating economic and social value. By making investments in, for example, local supply chain capacity and growing local markets, the Foundation met the company's required investment returns while simultaneously achieving social goals. This approach became known as creating shared value, promoted by leading management strategy theorists like Michael Porter (Porter and Kramer 2011).

It is always important to hold to account those companies that espouse social and environmental values along with their philanthropy. Memories are long, as Nestlé, with its baby formula scandal, Union Carbide with Bhopal, and Monsanto with its continual battle over genetically manipulated organisms, will attest. There is disillusionment with the "greenwashing" of some company's environmental credentials and investments, with espoused green values being rhetorical rather than real. There is concern that the social contributions of CSR in some ways distract attention away from any damage a company is doing. There is no doubt that when companies wish to act philanthropically, they have to be fully and transparently committed.

Companies have long been concerned with the bodily and spiritual welfare of their workforce, and this has extended into the communities in which they operate. The Quaker families in Britain—such as Rowntree, Cadbury and Fry in chocolate, Lloyds and Barclays in banking, and Darby in iron and wool—were founded upon their religious notions of social engagement and mutual advancement (Freeman 2013). This bond between personal and social progress was partly altruistic and partly good business sense. It was also the case that the fundamental paradox between hardworking Quaker business efficiency and distaste of material prosperity (Quakers believe personal wealth is corrosive to society and individuals) was to an extent alleviated by philanthropy. It was recognized that opportunities to create economic value increase when the society from which they emerge is better engaged in and rewarded by their realization. The Lever brothers, who created the soap company that later became Unilever, epitomized this belief: they were social reformers, insisting on shorter working days and health benefits for workers.

Upon her marriage in 1856, Caroline Colman, wife of the owner of the eponymous mustard company, became an active philanthropist. Prochaska (1990) tells of how she supported the local hospital and Sunday school, and various national charities, including the Bible Society, the London Missionary Society and the RSPCA. She provided technical classes for up to 200 men and sewing and cooking classes for women. The inexhaustible Mrs. Colman "hired sick visitors and nurses for (the company workers), provided a blanket and parcel distribution and at Christmas distributed hampers and works' almanacs of her own design. She established or oversaw a home for girls, a lending library, refreshment rooms at the factory, a milk scheme for children, mothers' meetings, a medical club, a sick benefit society with 500 members, a clothing club with 960 members and almshouses for pensioners".

The involvement with the workforce and community was also seen in Continental Europe. In Germany, the Carl-Zeiss-Stiftung aims for economic security of the firm, promotion of research and training and the development of the precision engineering sector, and to be socially responsible to its employees and "advancement in community facilities for the good of the working people of Jena".

One of the greatest philanthropic companies is Tata, the Indian multi-national conglomerate. The company was founded by Jamsetji Tata in 1868. Mahatma Gandhi is reputed to have said that the Tatas represent the spirit of adventure, and the journey of the Tatas has been highly adventurous, with great successes and substantial failures and setbacks (see e.g. Lala 2006). Yet throughout its history it has maintained its practices of giving back to the community and showing concern for the welfare of employees. It still retains much of the philosophy of its founder, Jamsetji, and the Tata's Parsi religion, with its emphasis on philanthropy, continues to remain highly influential. Jamsetji Tata wrote in, 1895: "we started on sound and straightforward business principles, considering the interests of the shareholders our own, and the health and welfare of the employees the sure foundation of our prosperity". Practically, and as indicators of its approach, this philosophy was seen in the institution of a pension fund in 1886 and paying accident compensation in 1895. To illustrate how far ahead of the times this was, WH Smith was one of the first British companies to operate a pension scheme and it began in 1894. Tata introduced the eight-hour working day in 1912, 36 years before it was mandated by the government, and maternity benefit 18 years before it was introduced by national law and provided an example to other companies.

This concern for employees was extended to broad Indian society. The major way the Tatas give back is through a series of trusts established by leading members of the family. One of these trusts was established in 1918 and another in 1932, and their intention is to promote the educational, social and scientific infrastructure in India. These trusts own two-thirds of the Tata company, and profits are invested to create a capital fund and to disperse grants. These trusts have supported a large range of some of the best known, and some less known, scientific, educational, medical and cultural institutions in India.

Other companies of more recent vintage build philanthropic giving into their fabric from their beginning. Atlassian is an Australian software company that was launched in 2002, and a few years later its two founders pledged to donate 1% of annual profits, 1% of employee time, and 1% of company equity to charity. At the time, this wasn't worth much, but now the company employs over 2000 and has reached a market capitalization of $10 billion. The two entrepreneurs created a foundation to structure its donations, which annually exceeds over $10 million and over 22,000 hours of staff time, and have been directed to causes such as preparing disadvantaged youth for the workforce of the future, and encouraging reading in developing countries. Additionally, the company has donated over 50,000 licences of its software free to charities. In 2014, Atlassian joined with Salesforce and Rally Software to form Pledge 1%, an organization dedicated to encouraging firms to donate 1% of one or combinations of their equity, time, product or profit.[10] Salesforce, for example, has given more than $168 million in grants, over 2 million hours of community service, and provided product donations to more than 32,000 nonprofit organizations and higher education institutions. Over 500 companies signed the Pledge in its first year, and there are now over 3000 signatories. Scott Farquar, Atlassian's co-founder and CEO says the benefactions have had huge benefit to the recipients and to the company staff, who feel engaged and enthused through their giving back.

Companies give for a variety of reasons, including to meet the expectations of their staff and the communities of which they are a part. They can gain beneficial public relations, and some may give for that purpose alone. They can also contribute valuable business expertise and organizational skills to their giving. Pledge 1%, for example, is structured in such a way as to make its joining and participating as simple and easy as possible.

As another example of the contribution of business, the Global Business Coalition for Women's Economic Empowerment is an initiative, led by Professor Linda Scott at Oxford University, involving companies including ExxonMobil Foundation, Coca-Cola, Goldman Sachs, Marks & Spencer, Mondleléz, Mastercard, PwC, Qualcomm, Wireless Reach and Walmart (Scott 2017). It is based on the precept that women's economic empowerment, so important for national development, needs to involve business. Nearly all the companies have a philanthropic effort trying to integrate women—as workers, customers, and suppliers—into their businesses. Scott describes how the reach of these companies is enormous, geographically, and in sectors including agriculture, manufacturing, digital communications and finance. She says their complex organizational and delivery structures—involving logistics, transportation, procurement, job training, recruitment, marketing and sales, government relations, financing and loans and digital security—allow them to engage with women in many roles.

It is because of their reach and distinctive capabilities and infrastructure that companies can be such important contributors, and partners with governments, foundations and individuals, in the conduct of philanthropy.

Attracting and Using Philanthropy

It has been seen that it can be challenging for philanthropists wishing to give their money away effectively. Attracting, accepting and effectively using benefaction also poses significant difficulties, especially for innovative and risky projects. How do you establish the most attractive proposals for funding, and identify the most likely donors with whom you can build trusting relationships? How do you ensure that benefactions do not redirect the purpose of the organization? How do you balance different sources of funding, and maintain good relationships with diverse contributors?

There are differences in approach between different types of beneficiaries. Philanthropy takes different forms, for example, amongst museums, art galleries and the performing arts. Art galleries may encourage philanthropists to buy particular paintings or sculptures to adorn collections. In museums, the attraction to donors often lies with the expertise of the people working in them and the quality of their exhibits. Theatres may attract sponsorships for particular shows and concerts. There are, however, some commonalities. Philanthropy funds innovative new departures and experiments, and helps shares their risks. It also enables leverage from government: it is easier to raise funds from government if philanthropy contributes significantly—usually more than 50%—of the costs of new initiatives. Furthermore, by encouraging more people to attend arts institutions and their events, philanthropy is building their sustainability by attracting new audiences that might not otherwise have patronized them, but will do so in future. In this way, as well as supporting the range and scope—i.e. the *supply*—of artistic organizations, philanthropy can also build *demand* for the arts.

Suzanne Miller, an internationally respected museum director, provides a number of insights into establishing and building sustainable relationships with donors.

First, be clear about the strengths of the organization you represent, its needs, potential and priorities. Have a clearly articulated vision and strategy.

Second, identify potential donors. This involves researching the strategies and plans of foundations, companies and individuals, exploring where there might be commonalties.

Third, search from within this set for donors with shared values and opportunities to build mutual trust. Donors respond better to ideas than to needs. Finding out about those shared values and ideas of the future involves considerable time and effort, researching corporate and family histories and documents. Philanthropy starts, she argues, with those shared values, and without them there cannot be the quality of the relationship that is necessary. In the past, she contends, there was a tendency to accept any gifts, but now there is the confidence to ensure they comply with the purpose and values of the organization.

Fourth, negotiate the relationship. This can be time-consuming, and should involve a lengthy conversation about shared objectives. During these conversations, misapprehensions can be cleared up and sometimes it becomes obvious that other partners may be best for both parties. This process also involves understanding where actual decision-making power lies in donor and beneficiary. The real costs and risks of donations need to be appreciated. The cost of a donation does not just lie with a gift itself and may, for example, include the costs of curating, displaying, storing and insuring exhibits. Donors need to be clear about the rights of the beneficiary, such as its ability at a later stage to dispose of a gift or renegotiate naming rights. At this stage, it is important to ensure the staff of the beneficiary are fully informed about the negotiations, there is a transparent process around them, and everyone in the organization is clear about the objectives of the relationship and have the opportunity to air their views about it.

Fifth, manage and maintain the relationship. This involves deep appreciation of the motives of the philanthropists, which Suzanne says is never seeking "grovelling gratefulness", but rather the mutual respect that emerges when shared values and high trust produce great outcomes. Beneficiaries need to be clear about what the return on investment is to philanthropists. Philanthropists want to contribute to the public good, and also find value in the social connections they forge with other like-minded donors. When they have a sense of ownership of the outcomes of their donations, philanthropists often encourage friends and acquaintances to also contribute. There needs to be sensitive understanding of the idiosyncratic expectations of donors: some may prefer public events, others are very private. All need to be continually informed and updated about the outcomes of their benefactions.

There are many good practices in managing these relationships. They include having highly skilled "development" or liaison staff. There may be a different skillset for managing individual, corporate or foundation philanthropists. Senior staff need to be trained in dealing with philanthropists, through mentoring and increasingly involving staff in external relationships as their careers progress. These staff members need to have a thorough understanding of the organization they represent. Events with donors need to be professionally organized such that information is effectively collected and captured about potential donors and existing donor satisfaction. Recognition is also needed for those behind the scenes who make invaluable contributions to the smooth running of the relationship. Suzanne, for example, organizes events to thank donor's personal assistants.

Suzanne emphasizes that effective philanthropy is never transactional, and always about the relationship. These relationships can evolve as friendships, and this can involve many different elements. On one level, it may involve "going to an awful lot of Christmas parties", but on the other addressing serious issues such as when donors are concerned whether their children share their values and how to negotiate the delicate balance of respecting the objectives of the next generation, and desire to continue to support the causes the donor believe in.

As well as involving professional fundraising personnel within organizations, many prospective beneficiaries hire expert external agencies to assist develop their strategies, processes and practices for increasing benefactions. Companies, such as Marts and Lundy, have developed significant capabilities and reputations for guiding better approaches to philanthropy.

CONSTRUCTING CAMPAIGNS

The search for benefaction often takes the form of a campaign. Campaigns have a long history, but in recent years fundraising has developed into a much more coordinated and professionalized activity. They are commonplace in many countries. The purpose of campaigns is to raise awareness of the level of giving required to achieve a particular goal and to broaden the base of support from a wider number of people. They also help institutions improve their credibility for fundraising by providing visibility for particular priorities associated with their mission. Campaigns can create urgency and focus for fundraising, both within an institution and across a broad community supporting the purposes of the institution, especially towards exciting and innovative initiatives.

In a common form, campaigns have several elements, including a "Quiet Phase" and a "Public Phase" over a period of 10 years. The Quiet

Phase takes the first 5 or 6 years and is used to generate about 50% of the overall amount required, before the campaign is launched publicly. Many organizations set the dates for their campaigns once they know the level of fundraising likely in the Quiet Phase and once detailed institutional priorities have been decided. This provides time for producing a "Case for Support" for the Public Phase and to create a structure for the campaign, including the allocation of internal resources. The Public Phase is usually only launched once an anchor donor has been identified and can be named.

The amount sought in a campaign is determined by the requirements of the institution's priorities for funding, and this often requires benchmarking against similar organizations. Ask for too little and your organization might seem to lack importance or ambition; ask for too much and you might fail to achieve your target during the Public Phase, or others might appear more attractive propositions. The purpose of the giving has to be clear, and its attractions and rewards to donors, clearly articulated. Donors often wish to know the success of the campaign to-date, and who else has donated. Beneficiaries have been known to retrospectively reallocate previously donated funds into the rubric of the campaign to demonstrate its currency. The number of potential donors required within particular identified financial bands of donation needs to be calculated in order to reach the target. Some institutions operate in continuous or rolling modes of campaigning, although campaign staff often move on to another institution after completion of a particular campaign and institutions recruit a different team to start the next one.

Whatever the institution receiving donations, be it museum, university, hospital or charity, their employees need to be involved in determining, and active in promoting, the strategic vision of the institution and its need for benefactions. Employees should be helpful and supportive in identifying, cultivating, and managing the relationships with donors, and appreciate the needs of their institution as well as their own or their immediate team or department's requirements. At the same time, those professionals leading the fundraising efforts need to fully appreciate the culture and practices of the institution they are representing. Campaigns need highly visible champions, such as famous employees or associated high-profile personalities, but work best when everyone in the organization champions the cause.

Wary of becoming overly reliant on limited sources and potential distortions to missions, institutions also need to be clear about the balance they are seeking between giving from foundations, corporations and very wealthy individuals, and smaller donations from a larger population. The latter can include, for example, voluntary donations from museum visitors, or contributions from university alumni or hospital patients. These help to counterbalance the influence of large donors.

Dependence

It is argued that some philanthropic giving can induce forms of dependence on the part of the recipient. These concerns range from the conviction in outlets such as *Brietbart News* that the liberalism of some American philanthropists is contributing to the mandating of welfare supports to purposefully constrain individual freedoms, to the more measured unease of development economists arguing a nation's reliance on international aid diminishes its incentives towards their advance and self-sufficiency.

Philanthropy aims to deal with the causes of problems, and this might imply building capacity to continually negate or remove their source. Dependence may reduce the incentive to achieve this. Renowned author Paul Theroux refers to "telescopic philanthropy", a term used by Charles Dickens to describe focussing on problems from afar, and how it might result in good intentions being ill-informed or having unseen adverse consequences.[11] Theroux uses the personal example of his early career teaching in Malawi, where part of his role was training local teachers. He returned 40 years later to find a continued paucity of Malawian, and many ex-patriot, teachers. Why bother training locals, he asks, when there is a continual supply of volunteer teachers from wealthy overseas countries?

Robert Merton's law (Merton 1936) of unintended consequences has powerful implications for philanthropic giving, when people's whole lifestyles can be adversely affected by decisions made in good faith. Improving water supplies in impoverished rural villages is a laudable aim, for example, but researchers at the Universities of Bristol and Addis Ababa found that this could increase their populations to unsustainable levels such that the healthiest and boldest people emigrate to cities, and often to destitution in slums. Their study of 1280 rural Ethiopian households showed that the installation of taps, which avoids women's back-breaking work of carrying water from wells and dramatically reduces child mortality, made the likelihood of young adults migrating to cities increase threefold.[12]

The implication for philanthropy, and the model pursued by the most impactful philanthropic organizations, is to be cautious about importing solutions from different contexts and being attuned to local conditions and unintended consequences.

NOTES

1. Cap Gemini, World Wealth Report 2017.
2. https://wellcome.ac.uk.
3. Stephen Foley, "Sean Parker: Hacker Philanthropist", *Financial Times*, May 2, 2016.
4. https://www.bloomberg.org/.
5. "Giving Like Michael Bloomberg: 'Find One Small Thing'", *New York Times*, Paul Sullivan, May 20, 2016.
6. *The Economist*, March 10, 2018.
7. Foundation Center, 2017.
8. "The Wolfson Foundation: 1955–2015, Sixty Years of Philanthropy", London, The Wolfson Foundation.
9. "Charities Are Becoming More Professional", *The Economist*, September 30, 2017.
10. https://pledge1percent.org/.
11. https://www.barrons.com/articles/africaaposs-aid-mess-1385805908.
12. http://journals.plos.org/plosone/article?id=10.1371/journal.pone. 0048708.

REFERENCES

Acs, Z. (2013). *Why Philanthropy Matters*. Princeton, NJ: Princeton University Press.

Callahan, D. (2017). *The Givers: Wealth, Power, and Philanthropy in a New Gilded Age*. New York: Knopf.

Crocker, R. (2005). "Nothing More for Men's Colleges": The Educational Philanthropy of Mrs. Russell Sage. In A. Walton (Ed.), *Women and Philanthropy in Education*. Bloomington: Indiana University Press.

Dodgson, M., Gann, D., & Phillips, N. (Eds.). (2014). *The Oxford Handbook of Innovation Management*. Oxford: Oxford University Press.

Freeman, M. (2013). Quakers, Business and Philanthropy. In S. Angell & B. Dandelion (Eds.), *The Oxford Handbook of Quaker Studies*. Oxford: Oxford University Press.

Giridharadas, A. (2018). *Winners Take All: The Elite Charade of Changing the World*. New York: Penguin Random House.

Jaumont, F. (2016). *Unequal Partners: American Foundations and Higher Education Development in Africa*. New York: Palgrave Macmillan.

Lala, R. (2006). *The Creation of Wealth: The Tatas from the 19th to the 21st Century*. New Delhi: Penguin/Portfolio.

Loebl, S. (2010). *America's Medicis: The Rockefellers and Their Astonishing Cultural Legacy*. New York: Harper.

Mayer, J. (2016). *Dark Money: How a Secretive Group of Billionaires Is Trying to Buy Political Control in the US*. Melbourne: Scribe Publications.

McGoey, L. (2015). *No Such Thing as a Free Gift*. London: Verso.

Merton, R. (1936). The Unanticipated Consequences of Purposive Social Action. *American Sociological Review, 1*(6), 894–904.

Offer, A. (1997). Between the Gift and the Market: The Economy of Regard. *Economic History Review, 50*(3), 450–476.

Ostrower, F. (1997). *Why the Wealthy Give: The Culture of Elite Philanthropy*. Princeton, NJ: Princeton University Press.

Perkins, A. (2011). *Edwin Rogers Embree: The Julius Rosenwald Fund, Foundation Philanthropy, and American Race Relations*. Bloomington: Indiana University Press.

Porter, M., & Kramer, M. (2011). Creating Social Value. *Harvard Business Review, 89*(1/2), 62–77.

Prochaska, F. (1990). Philanthropy. In F. Thompson (Ed.), *The Cambridge Social History of Britain* (pp. 1750–1950). Cambridge: Cambridge University Press.

Reich, R. (2013, March/April). What Are Foundations For? *Boston Review.*

Schervish, P. (2003, November 14). *Hyperagency and High-Tech Donors: A New Theory of the New Philanthropists*. New Haven: Boston College Social Welfare Research Institute.

Scott, L. (2017). *Private Sector Engagement with Women's Economic Empowerment: Lessons Learned from Years of Practice*. Saïd Business School, University of Oxford.

Skocpol, T. (2016). Politics Symposium: Why Political Scientists Should Study Organized Philanthropy. *PS Political Science and Politics, 49*(3), 433–436.

Tierney, T., & Fleishma, J. (2012). *Give Smart: Philanthropy That Gets Results*. New York: Public Affairs.

Twersky, F. (2014, Summer). The Artful Juggler. *Stanford Social Innovation Review.*

Wolf Ditkoff, S., & Grindle, A. (2017, September–October). Audacious Philanthropy. *Harvard Business Review*, pp. 110–118.

CHAPTER 5

Controversies and Future Challenges

Abstract This chapter reflects on the controversies and challenges of philanthropy. It addresses the issues of the application of new technologies to philanthropy, such as AI, blockchains and cryptocurrencies. It considers new metrics and tools for assessing the impact of philanthropy. The importance of government and regulation is discussed. The manner in which philanthropy is a global phenomenon is described. A future research agenda is outlined.

Keywords Controversies in philanthropy · Philanthropy and new technology · Philanthropy and AI · Philanthropy and blockchain · Philanthropy and cryptocurrencies · New metrics for philanthropy · Philanthropy and government regulation · Global philanthropy · Future research agenda for philanthropy

BRINGING ABOUT CHANGE

We began by posing the question of whether philanthropy is society's hope of the future or a fifth column, and have shown that it can be both. Its contribution essentially remains an open research question. There are circumstances where philanthropy can be a powerfully positive force for

© The Author(s) 2020
M. Dodgson and D. Gann, *Philanthropy,
Innovation and Entrepreneurship*,
https://doi.org/10.1007/978-3-030-38017-5_5

innovation and social progress, and yet it can also fail to deliver on expectations, and have detrimental social consequences. In this final chapter, we turn to some of the issues that will determine philanthropy's contributions in the future and whether and how it will meet the entrepreneurial ambitions of philanthropic donors in bringing about change.

INNOVATION AND TECHNOLOGY

Philanthropy can support and deliver innovations, and new innovations and technologies have the potential to profoundly affect the conduct and impact of philanthropy. The study of innovation and technological change tells us about the challenges in the diffusion and use of technology, and the dangers of "technological determinism". Nonetheless, with sufficient attention to the human and organizational issues surrounding innovation, it can profoundly affect the practice of philanthropy. Furthermore, the kinds of digital technologies that will be particularly influential may be especially appealing to the Millennial generation of philanthropists.

The practices of philanthropic giving have not in the past been noted for their innovativeness. Prochaska (1990) notes wryly that innovation was the hallmark of philanthropy in Britain in the nineteenth century, as with increasing demands made on limited resources, great ingenuity was shown in extracting funds. There are examples of innovation in the sector, such as demanding funds are matched by recipients or governments, or establishing fixed term for foundation trustees, and as we have seen, philanthropy can induce innovation. Yet there is also conservatism in the sector.

One cause of such conservatism is the cost of failure. People's lives can be adversely affected, sometimes dramatically. Yet failure is an unavoidable aspect of innovation, and if philanthropy is to be truly ambitious and innovative, mistakes will be made. As shown in the example of Rockefeller's Yellow Fever vaccine, the history of philanthropic investments is replete with failures. Carnegie famously built a Peace Palace in The Hague, now home to the International Court of Justice, and funded the Carnegie Endowment for International Peace, neither of which had much influence in preventing the First World War. The immediacy and breadth of potential communications about failure in social media are likely to be more of a disincentive to experiments today, although such technology may also provide opportunities for experimentation.

Where there is conservatism and reticence to change, there are opportunities for disruption. Much of the future disruption in philanthropy will occur through technological change. Digital technologies, such as crowd-funding of philanthropic initiatives, can attract investments in highly innovative ideas. Start-up organizations, such as Epic Foundation, are using technology to be disruptive.[1] Started by Alexandre Mars, a French entrepreneur, Epic uses technology to directly connect donors and charities, especially those concerned with children and young people. The foundation has an app that allows donors immediate information on the organizations to which they have contributed. A series of virtual reality films give donors a more immersive experience of where their money is going and the impact it has.

One of the greatest consequences of the ubiquity of digital technologies is the increased availability of data, and the capacity to analyse it. The Australian philanthropist, Andrew Forrest, who apart from funding universities, aboriginal employment, and an anti-slavery campaign, amongst other causes, realizes the importance of data in the search for the better treatment of cancer. He funded the creation of the Universal Cancer Databank, a global data-sharing project.[2] The Databank aims to gather medical information on cancer patients around the world and combine it with individual genome sequencing and profiling. Cancer patients are encouraged to hand over their health records to the databank, with their privacy assured, so that it can be shared by researchers across the world in ways that were previously impossible. The first signatory in the Databank was Baroness Tessa Jowell who, suffering from brain cancer, expressed the hope that by sharing her data, there would be faster discovery of better treatments.

Although it is advisable to be cautious when predicting the future impact of emerging technologies, three technologies likely to have significant consequences for philanthropy are Artificial Intelligence (AI), blockchain and cryptocurrencies.

Artificial Intelligence (AI) has the potential to overcome bias and enhance prediction, both of which are crucial for philanthropy. AI could possibly screen applications for support and grants, revealing data about the applicants and their likelihood of achieving stated objectives, and assess whether these objectives comply with the values and strategies of the donor. The technology can conceivably remove embedded biases in decision-making. Chatbots could be used to assist applications, improving efficiencies by guiding applicants. AI might be used for real time reporting on performance, and potentially flag when problems are emerging. The predictive power of AI is being used, for example, in identifying when famines are likely to occur (assisted, perhaps, by geospatial cameras or drones recording crop performance). Preparations can then be made to deal with famines before people suffer their consequences. The Famine Action Mechanism, a global initiative involving the World Bank, United Nations, International Committee of the Red Cross, Microsoft, Google and Amazon Web Services, is exploring a model to predict famine that is being tested in five countries.[3]

Predictive analytics could also potentially be used in humanitarian financing, impact assessment, predicting movement of people (refugees, migrants and internally displaced people), improving supportive supply chains, identifying poor performers (helping allocate funding more appropriately) and rethinking labour costs (i.e. how many field staff need to be where). The UN Office for the Coordination of Humanitarian Affairs is opening a centre on predictive analytics, and receives donations from private individuals.

On the downside of AI, given the concerns about its potential misuse, some philanthropists, such as Steve Schwarzman and Nicolas Berggruen, are funding research into the ethical issues associated with the technology. The former has made very substantial donations in this field to universities such as MIT and Oxford, but while the focus of the funded research is ethics, controversies surround the source of these donations.[4]

Blockchain technology has the potential to significantly affect the structures and practices of giving. Transactions through blockchain are done peer-to-peer, transferring resources and information directly from one party to another. This means that trusted third parties—such as banks, and potentially intermediaries such as charities—could be replaced by clever programming and cryptography in systems so secure that they can prevent fraud, misappropriation, leaking, tampering or hacking. Transactions can use cryptocurrencies such as Bitcoin, or with official fiat currencies (government legal tender) which are represented on the blockchain by tokens.

Blockchain can potentially provide a number of benefits. It can verify identities in a secure way, to ensure people and organizations are who they say they are, reducing opportunities for fraud. By dis-intermediating payments and transfers, transaction costs could be reduced resulting in a larger portion of donations reaching the recipient or beneficiary. The transparent nature of blockchain transactions means that donors could trace where their money has gone, rather than losing it in opaque internal charity or foundation processes. Donations made to a particular hospital, for example, can be made directly, without having to be processed by intermediaries such as Ministries of Health. This brings its own dangers, as donors may have especial concern for particular diseases, while government ministries have responsibility for their nation's entire range of health concerns.

Operating costs of charities and foundations could also be dramatically reduced through blockchain technology. For foundations that pay expensive intermediary fees, operate with high overheads and use opaque internal processes, blockchain offers a solution to reduce costs and improve transparency.

Saving costs through using Blockchain

A UK fund management platform called Disberse uses blockchain technology to transfer fiat money from UK charities to overseas charities.[5] Working with the START Network, a group of 42 aid agencies across five continents that aims to deliver more effective emergency aid, Disberse piloted a transfer of money from the UK, through blockchain, to a charity in Swaziland. By skipping the legacy banking system and the normal currency conversion processes, Disberse saved 2.5% in fees and the entire process was visible and traceable. The savings made in this particular transaction paid for three girls from Swaziland to attend school for one year.

The World Food Programme's Building Blocks project uses blockchain to support aid distribution amongst Syrian refugees in Jordan.[6] By cutting out an intermediary bank they were previously using to transfer funds to refugees, the World Food Programme claims a 98% reduction in local bank fees. The majority of savings came from not having to do separate reconciliation and auditing of the bank's records as they already had their own immutable records stored on the blockchain.

A feature of blockchain technology called "smart contracts" offers the potential to automate donation processes, and even potentially take over some of the governance of philanthropic foundations. Smart contracts involve contractual obligations being written into computer code which will trigger and self-execute once all of the conditions of the contract are met. Smart contracts could embed philanthropic clauses by stipulating that if certain conditions are met, money will automatically be transferred to the donor's chosen cause. This is essentially codifying and automating the wishes of philanthropists, saving them time and money in the process.

Smart contracts could even make the substantive philanthropic decision—the choice for which cause to support—on behalf of the donor or business. It can do this through using analysed data, predetermined parameters and AI. Money ear-marked for donation could sit in escrow until a cause or need becomes so great that it triggers the smart contract. Funds ear-marked for disaster relief, for example, could be triggered after an event such as an earthquake. Further parameters could be added to the smart contract including that funds will only be released if X amount of people are affected, and/or donations from other entities fall short. Funds could even potentially be triggered pre-emptively, for example, when dam levels reach a certain low and rainfall drops to a predetermined point. Donations could be made available before the drought starts taking lives.

This is an important consideration because donations can take a long time to reach beneficiaries. Processes such as human assessment and legacy banking systems can delay funds reaching the recipients, and philanthropists supporting emergency causes such as disaster relief, disease outbreak and refugee crises will value the immediacy that blockchain can offer.

Smart contracts could eventually govern more and more of a foundation's or charity's operations, perhaps becoming what are known as Decentralized Autonomous Organizations, which are entities entirely run by rules which have been put into code and stored in smart contracts.

Cryptocurrencies have the potential to affect the way philanthropy is delivered and the pool of philanthropists. There are hundreds of cryptocurrencies, and cryptoassets as of January 2018 have a total market capitalization of $550 billion.

A foundation or charity may accept funds in its cryptocurrency (digital) form. To do this, they would have to download a "wallet" which is essentially a cryptocurrency account. With a wallet, it only takes several clicks of a button and a few seconds to transfer money from the crypto-philanthropist to the recipient. The recipient can then use the money in cryptocurrency form (by paying it onwards to another entity accepting cryptocurrency), or they can use an exchange service to convert it into local fiat currency such as Sterling or US dollars. However, many countries have uncertain and changing laws and regulations regarding the purchase, trading and exchange of cryptocurrencies. To avoid falling foul of the law in these countries the crypto-philanthropist would have to exchange their cryptocurrency into fiat currency themselves, and then use the normal means (such as a bank) to send onwards to the beneficiary. Care, however, needs to be taken in securing such wallets, as they can be the target of hacking.

The dramatic increase in the value of cryptocurrencies has left many, particularly early adopters, unexpectedly rich, spawning a new generation of crypto-philanthropists. Due to the anonymous and pseudonymous nature of cryptocurrencies, not a lot is known about who these donors are or where the money is going. Some publicly known crypto-wealthy include the Winklevoss twins (of Facebook fame), Vitalik Buterin, the creator of Ethereum, and Jed McCaleb, the creator of the cryptocurrency Ripple, who was momentarily richer than Mark Zuckerberg. Data suggests that about 94% of Bitcoin wealth is held by men, and some estimate that 95% of that wealth is held by 4% of the owners. It is likely, therefore, that the typical crypto-philanthropist is a millennial-aged man with a technology background and libertarian values. Some notable public donations indicate that crypto-philanthropy has a different agenda to traditional and even hacker philanthropy, and it may be that the appetite for the crypto-wealthy to give away part of their profits is as volatile as the value of the cryptocurrency itself.

One of the first sizeable donations made with cryptocurrency was in 2014 by Jed McCaleb. He donated $500,000 of Ripple's cryptocurrency to the Machine Intelligence Research Institute: the largest single donation ever made to them. If the Institute had held onto the cryptocurrency and not exchanged it into fiat currency until January 2018, this donation would be worth $19,000,000. Such is the risk for beneficiaries of cryptocurrency: one day a $1,000,000 cryptocurrency donation could be worth $6,000,000 and the next day $100,000.

There are a number of reasons why the crypto-wealthy donate to philanthropic causes. Although not uniformly applied, governments around the world are defining cryptoassets as taxable income, and crypto-owners are often liable to pay capital gains tax on their profits. This incentivizes the crypto-wealthy to offload part of their profits. Fidelity Charitable Trust, for example, received $22 million in Bitcoin donations in 2017.

Other than tax, some crypto-wealthy are giving profits away simply because they have made large amounts of money in very little time for very little effort. According to "Pine" an anonymous crypto-philanthropist: "Because once you have enough money, money doesn't matter". "Pine" set up the Pineapple Fund which promised to donate

$86 million of crypto-wealth. Pine accepts emails from charities pitching for funding in an anonymous and fully digital process of screening. There are a variety of beneficiaries: 28 of which are new organizations established within the last decade. While there are many donations made to traditional causes such as education and health, there is a clear support for tech-savvy charities and causes supporting digital privacy and open-source technology. Several donations were made to psychedelics medical research, and both the Pineapple Fund and Vitalik Buterin made sizeable donations of several million dollars to an anti-ageing medical research facility.

It is possible to consider the crypto-wealthy as ideal philanthropists for funding riskier and more entrepreneurial ventures. They have seen first-hand the benefits of taking such risks. But with the exception of the Pineapple Fund, it is difficult to track the activities of crypto-philanthropists. The crypto-community tend to communicate via internet forums such as Reddit, Telegram and Slack, and often speak in a unique crypto-language. Trolls flood these forums so it is difficult to tell who is legitimate and who is a fake. Fundraisers and foundations will have to learn to navigate this new arena in order to identify and appeal to a new type of crypto-wealthy.

All these new technologies, including, amongst others, crowdfunding, data analytics, AI, blockchain and cryptocurrencies, provide opportunities and threats for philanthropists. There are, however, considerable challenges in increasing the former and avoiding the latter, especially it might be argued in more traditional organizations. A survey on Foundation governance, undertaken for the Center for Effective Philanthropy, found that while 95% of Foundation boards included experts in investing and in accounting, only 39% had experts in technology.[7]

New Metrics and Tools

In addition to technologies such as blockchain, the explosion in the availability of data, and the ability to process and display it, is helping make better decisions through improved metrics and tools. The international diffusion of 6 billion smart phones, for example, provides opportunities for tracking the movement of people, including refugees. Using data can help optimize philanthropic decision-making, including supporting the conduct of randomized control trials to measure the impact of interventions. The greater availability of data and ease of its interpretation can aid the transparency of decisions and decision-making processes. Crowd-sourcing can be used to help identify priorities for giving and assessing impact.

Beneficiaries as well as benefactors gain through better availability of data. The 360Giving initiative is establishing a data standard that allows grant givers to share information between themselves as well as potential recipients in an open, machine-readable and easily comparable manner. The use of open data allows donors and recipients to comprehensively search for existing or competing projects, allowing for the better sharing of information and preventing duplication.

Caroline Fiennes of Giving Evidence in an article in *Nature* lists a raft of questions yet to be answered about effective giving.[8] These include *size* of grants, as it is not clear whether large grants have proportionately greater impact or whether small grants are easier to apply for. There are questions of *scope* and the relative effectiveness of broad vs narrow focus, and *time* and the appropriate duration of grants. She argues there is still uncertainty of the merits of funders *partnering* with others, the extent to which they become *involved* in the work that is supported, and the *selection* process, i.e. should they be solicited from particular parties or open to all, and when it comes to selection what is the best balance between submissions, peer review and interviews?

Fiennes makes a plea for a more scientific philanthropy and suggests that answering three rather simple questions can provide useful insights for any donor. First, how many grants achieve their goals (the donor's hit rate)? Second, what proportion of funds are devoted to activities such as preparing proposals or reports for the donor? Third, how satisfied are the recipients with the donor's process? Reflecting how poor many donors are at assessing their effectively she suggests that recording the goal of every grant and tracking whether these goals were met would be a big step forward. All these questions may appear obvious, but the way they need to be posed points to their continuing currency.

GOVERNMENT AND REGULATIONS

Views on the relationships between philanthropists and governments range from those who would replace government spending with as much philanthropic giving as possible, and vice versa, to those who recognize their symbiotic connections. Michael Bloomberg is in the latter camp and suggests philanthropy is not an alternative to government, but a way of emboldening it. As "society's risk capital", philanthropy can experiment, test and prototype ideas, that governments with all their resources and reach can subsequently implement. Ideally, in this view, relationships should draw synergistically on the innovativeness and responsiveness of philanthropy and scale of resources and authority of government. The early campaigns against slavery and child cruelty, for example, recognized that no matter how energetic their activities, results depended on changes in government policy. If experiments are to be scaled-up, engagement with government is crucial and many philanthropists are concerned with influencing government policy.

The relationship between philanthropy and government is one of continual adjustment. The importance of philanthropy in the UK in the mid- to late-2010s, for example, has to be assessed in an era of austerity when the government was reticent to invest in public goods, especially in those whose likely returns exceeds the electoral cycle. These adjustments can involve significant tensions over responsibilities and sometimes very divergent practices between government and philanthropy. This divergence can be extreme: In colonial Australia, alongside the brutality meted out to the indigenous population by the government there was also private philanthropic concern for aboriginal land rights going back to the 1830s.

The attitudes and approaches to government by philanthropists are influenced by their political opinions, and by simple pragmatic concerns. As an example of the latter, one perennial fear of philanthropists is that giving to a particular cause, for example an orchestra or a school, may encourage the government to withdraw its funding. As shown by Ostrower (1997), philanthropists strongly adhere to the view they are better at making decisions than governments. On the political dimension, Skocpol (2016) argues that "conservative foundations and wealthy donors have been patient in giving sustained support to right-wing think tanks, whereas liberal donors and foundations have followed a stop-start pattern, leading to many failed efforts to build an equally powerful network". That is not to say that liberal or left-wing philanthropists have had no voice in US politics, simply they have not been as effective in recent times. Whatever the political flavour of government, philanthropists often with markedly different views may need to cooperate with them in order to have the impact they are seeking.

One strongly held view amongst libertarian philanthropists is that state spending "crowds out" more efficient private investment. As noted earlier, some philanthropists believe this applies to government investment in science. Evidence suggests the opposite, with public investment actually attracting private investment.[9] Private investment in science could also lead governments to withdraw from important research areas. Governments, furthermore, have broad social responsibilities, so, for example, if medical research priorities are determined largely by a population of older White men with their particular health concerns, what implications does this have for those in different demographics, such as minority groups confronted by dissimilar health problems? This example illustrates the benefits of the symbiotic view of government–philanthropy connections.

The political nature of the discussion on philanthropy extends to the nature of its regulation. On this question, there are many voices for change, in for example increasing accountability and transparency and limiting political objectives, yet because groups representing divergent opinions are presently operating successfully, and display such strong emotional attachment to their giving, and with no pressing demands for change, there are many obstacles to amending regulatory regimes.

A Global Phenomenon

According to Capgemini's World Wealth Report in 2018, there were 18.1 million people in the world with at least $1 million in investable assets (i.e. not including the family home).[10] This increased from 11.0 million seven years previously. The pool of potential philanthropists is therefore increasing. The spread of these individuals is roughly equal in Asia-Pacific, North America and Europe, with a slightly smaller percentage in the rest of the world, mainly Latin America. The largest group comes from Asia-Pacific, but the largest individual country is the USA. Capgemini estimates that the wealth of this group of people around the world will exceed $100 trillion by 2025.

Philanthropy is believed by some to be best personified by Americans, but historically there has always been some ambiguity about the nationality of many of the better-known givers. Some of the greatest American philanthropists, such as Carnegie and Scripps, were born in and retained strong allegiance with Britain, Peabody spent most of his life in London, Getty lived in Britain, and Smithson, of Smithsonian Institution fame, never visited the USA. Sir Henry Wellcome, founder of the UK's largest foundation, was an American, and his wealth derived from research undertaken in his American laboratories. European philanthropists, such as the Mond family, always had a strongly international dimension to their giving.

Philanthropy is increasingly an international and internationalized phenomenon. The development of philanthropy in China, for example, continues apace. The state is increasingly allowing philanthropic contributions, albeit highly regulated. Wealthy Chinese are donating vast sums to good causes, but there is a question about the extent to which, unlike many of their Western counterparts, they are prepared to commit to addressing challenging social causes. Throughout Asia there is a continuing evolution in the debate on "the value proposition of civil society and the role of private citizens" (Shapiro 2018).

Philanthropists invest overseas to assist, to influence and promote understanding, and to change, and their welcome is commonly ranked in that order. As is probably the case in all philanthropic giving, it is most effective when it works with its recipients rather than imposes its view of what is needed.

One of the major future sources of philanthropic giving will be the growing middle classes in Asia, Latin America and Africa. These will not be high net worth individuals of the sort discussed in this book, and they will contribute smaller amounts that collectively have the potential to be greater in scale than those from the very wealthy. This source of funds is important in and of itself, but it also provides the opportunity, if sufficiently well-marshalled, to provide a balance to the wishes of a few key people, by representing the concerns and ambitions of a wider and more diverse population.

A Future Research Agenda

Philanthropy has become a focus of academic study, but not to the level its importance warrants. Despite its long history and massive scale, there are still many questions surrounding it, and the whole field is ripe for considerably more research. Skocpol, for example, suggests: "It is obvious that more empirical work is needed to explore macroscopic trends and trace the overall impact of foundation routines and donor practices in various policy realms". Anheier and Leat (2006), similarly call for greater research into the precise contributions of Foundations. There are, however, some strong research centres in universities such as Stanford and Indiana, and think tanks and lobbying groups such as the Center for Effective Philanthropy and National Committee for Responsive Philanthropy, that undertake research.[11] There is a European Research Network on Philanthropy with 175 members from 22 countries.

Nonetheless, the research that is undertaken is primarily US-focussed, and very little of it is high-impact, measured by subsequent citations or demonstrable impact on practice. There are also significant shortcomings in the research because of the category confusions noted earlier limiting comparisons and cumulative learning. Absent sufficient scholarly scrutiny and sound empirical evidence and many fundamental questions remain, for example, on whether philanthropic expenditure is wisely made, with clear measures of success; how foundations should be led, governed, supported, core funded and held to account; the key motives, methods and skills needed for giving and receiving and how these are changing; and whether governments receive adequate return or appropriate accountability for the tax benefits they provide. There is always room for better data, analysing trends. Other major questions include:

What are the consequences for civil society when philanthropic giving, rather than governments, determine priorities for social, scientific, cultural and humanitarian investments?

To what extent is philanthropy supporting risky, innovative endeavours that address the complex social problems that governments and large businesses are increasingly avoiding?

How do European, Asian and other international models of philanthropy differ from that found in America, and are they converging or diverging?

How are new technologies affecting the structures and practices of giving?

How is trust built and maintained in the ethics and probity of those giving and receiving benefactions, and how is it restored if trusting relationships are broken?

In what circumstances do private philanthropy, corporate philanthropy and government interventions work best individually and in combinations?

Answers to such questions require a genuinely interdisciplinary approach, drawing on broad-ranging academic knowledge and skills. Historians seek to understand the ways in which philanthropy has changed over time, and along with political scientists explore how it operates in specific national and temporal contexts. Sociologists, anthropologists and scholars of religion and culture help explain broader propensities to give. Philosophers can illuminate the tensions between philanthropy, justice and competing ethical priorities.

Questions posed by philosophers on the ethics of philanthropy
These questions are posed by Paul Woodruff, Professor of Ethics and American Society at University of Texas (Woodruff 2018)

> Why should one give? What is it that wealthy tightwads do not understand? Is generosity a virtue? Do we have duties to give? If we do, then clearly we will be in the wrong if we do not give. And a question follows: Are philanthropic duties narrow or wide? If narrow, these duties would be specific to particular causes and perhaps would require us to give specified amounts. How are the causes and amounts to be determined? But perhaps philanthropy is supererogatory—a good deed beyond the call of duty, earning merit when done, but not blame when left undone. What is the connection between philanthropy and altruism: can one be a selfish or self-interested philanthropist? How should philanthropists weight the values of various causes, such as religion, the arts, education, human rights, animal rights, and saving lives from hunger and disease? Is it wrong to give money to the arts when that money could have saved lives?

Psychologists help analysis of personal generosity, altruism and esteem. Economists provide insights into how giving is affected by changing economic and fiscal conditions and the ways in which it responds to incentives, a subject also of interest to behavioural psychologists. Political scientists, public policy experts and legal scholars provide views on formulating appropriate government policy and legal frameworks for philanthropy.

Business and innovation scholars provide insights into the entrepreneurial wealth creation underpinning philanthropy and good practice in its delivery and assessment of risk and impact. Management experts delve into the similarities and contrasts between public, private

and philanthropy governance and leadership and highlight the particular
hurdles of fundraising.

**Management challenges around the governance and organization
of philanthropic giving include**
Ensuring clarity and effective communication of vision and purpose.

Establishing clear criteria for giving, monitoring performance and measuring and assessing delivery against mission.

Creating the most effective organizational structures and operational procedures and practices, to ensure ethical standards and efficiency, without stultifying and overly expensive bureaucracy.

Deciding where to collaborate in delivery and provision of infrastructure.

Managing the flow of requests for funding/opportunities for giving.

Identifying, recruiting, training, developing and effectively utilizing trustees.

Constructing and operating the most effective committee structures, for example risk and remuneration.

Establishing the most effective working relationships between the trustees and senior leadership team, the Chair and the CEO, and where a main giver or family is concerned, their relationship with the foundation's trustees and senior management team.

The growing importance of philanthropy implies a requirement for a concomitant increase in the number of educational and training offerings in the field, and there are some indications this may be occurring. The Economist reports the number of courses at American universities in non-profit management and philanthropic studies rose from 284 in 1986 to 651 in 2016. In 1980, 8% of Harvard's Masters in Public Policy Government took jobs in the non-profit sector. By 2015 that had risen to around 30%.[12]

FINAL THOUGHTS

The scale and scope of philanthropy makes it a major contributor to social progress, but there are strong views on how assessing its importance and significance needs to be tempered with concerns about how the great wealth of some individuals should not be used to promote political partisanship, societal division and personal promotion and advance. It is evident that at a time when philanthropic giving is increasing, social inequalities are accelerating. The very first line of Andrew Carnegie's *Gospel of Wealth* reads: "The problem of our age is the proper administration of wealth, that the ties of brotherhood may still bind together the rich and poor in harmonious relationship". The problem of the age at the end of the nineteenth century, remains the problem of the age today.

It is widely held that resources from philanthropy need to directed to the areas of greatest need and towards producing the greatest impact. As John D. Rockefeller wrote in his autobiography in 1909:

> We must always remember that there is not enough money for the work of human uplift and that there never can be. How vitally important it is, therefore, that the expenditure should go as far as possible and be used with the greatest intelligence! (Rockefeller 2013)

Impact can be improved through collaboration between foundations and charities and between them and governments and the private sector. This not only adds scale in addressing problems, but extends the scope of distinctive and complementary capabilities brought to bear. In 2017, several signatories of the Giving Pledge agreed to pool resources in an initiative called Co-Impact.[13] This aims to increase the scale of resources available to tackle system-wide problems such as inequality and health, involving philanthropists, governments and international agencies. It also aims to prevent duplication of effort amongst foundations.

The crucial role for philanthropy, for many, is as an accelerant for innovation and risk-taking. In this view, it should encourage innovation, experiment, prototyping, testing and be tolerant of failure. As Reich (2019) contends, the goal of foundations should be "discovery", or long-time-horizon innovations that enhance democratic experimentalism. Philanthropy's greatest contribution to social advance and humanitarian causes is being active in places where government and corporations fear to tread.

For this to happen, government policies and regulations would need to be attuned to the innovation-supporting and risk-taking features of philanthropy. Taxation regimes should, to this purpose, encourage longer-term commitments and/or riskier investments, supporting patience and audacity, and provide consistency and continuity to ensure confidence in giving. Given the highly skewed influence of a small number of very wealthy givers, taxation regimes might be constructed to encourage greater giving of smaller amounts by less wealthy individuals to be more reflective of broader societal concerns.

There are calls for much greater independent research and evidence in "philanthropy studies", from philosophical questions on the ethics of giving to its practicalities. Research is needed into the effectiveness of giving, and the possibilities and consequences of unforeseen consequences and dependence. People are entitled to be sceptical of the motivations of individuals and corporations that extol the virtues of social cohesion and progress, yet energetically work to minimize their tax obligations in ways the general population cannot. The challenge is for the philanthropy sector to be innovative and responsive in the problems it addresses and accountable and transparent in the way it does so. There are advantages in innovation by philanthropists and innovation in philanthropy.

Few would argue against the view that philanthropic giving and receiving should be based on the principles of transparency and accountability. Its social legitimacy is enhanced when its decisions and decision-making processes are visible to all. While respecting an individual's desire for anonymity, if it is desired, donations should, it is argued, be readily visible to appropriate government authorities. Foundations and beneficiaries should, in this view, be public about their strategies, objectives and funding processes, and also their performance—the extent to which they meet their objectives.

The great good of which philanthropy is capable should be celebrated, but caution also needs to be exercised as to its possible harms. At its best, as well as addressing need, philanthropy builds social relationships by demonstrating mutual commitments to a better future amongst people in a fractured world.

NOTES

1. https://epic.foundation/.
2. https://ucd.eliminatecancer.org/.

3. https://www.worldbank.org/en/news/press-release/2018/09/23/
united-nations-world-bank-humanitarian-organizations-launch-innovative-
partnership-to-end-famine.
4. https://www.theguardian.com/commentisfree/2019/jun/22/ethics-fly-
out-window-oxford-university-when-big-donors-come-calling.
5. https://disberse.com/.
6. https://innovation.wfp.org/project/building-blocks.
7. http://www.effectivephilanthropy.org/wp-content/uploads/2015/10/
BenchmarkingFoundationGovernance2015.pdf.
8. Caroline Fiennes (2017). "We Need a Science of Philanthropy", *Nature*,
June 8, Vol. 546, p. 187.
9. The Economic Significance of the UK Science Base, Jonathan Haskel
Alan Hughes Elif Bascavusoglu-Moreau, UK Innovation Research Centre, March 2014.
10. https://worldwealthreport.com/.
11. https://cep.org/; https://www.ncrp.org/.
12. "Charities Are Becoming More Professional", *The Economist*, September
30, 2017.
13. https://co-impact.org/.

References

Anheier, H., & Leat, D. (2006). *Creative Philanthropy: Towards a New Philan-
thropy for the 21st Century*. London and New York: Routledge.
Ostrower, F. (1997). *Why the Wealthy Give: The Culture of Elite Philanthropy*.
Princeton, NJ: Princeton University Press.
Prochaska, F. (1990). Philanthropy. In F. Thompson (Ed.), *The Cambridge Social
History of Britain* (pp. 1750–1950). Cambridge: Cambridge University Press.
Reich, R. (2019). *Just Giving: Why Philanthropy Is Failing Democracy and How
It Can Do Better*. Princeton, NJ: Princeton University Press.
Rockefeller, J. (2013). *Random Reminiscenses of Men and Events*. Paperback
Bunko.
Shapiro, R. (2018). Asian Philanthropy Explained. In R. Shapiro, M.
Mirchandani, & H. Jang (Eds.), *Pragmatic Philanthropy: Asian Charity
Explained*. Singapore: Palgrave Macmillan.
Skocpol, T. (2016). Politics Symposium: Why Political Scientists Should Study
Organized Philanthropy. *PS Political Science and Politics, 49*(3), 433–436.
Woodruff, P. (2018). *The Ethics of Giving: Philosophers' Perspectives on Philan-
thropy*. New York: Oxford University Press.

Bibliography

Acs, Z. (2013). *Why Philanthropy Matters*. Princeton, NJ: Princeton University Press.

Adam, T. (1989 [2016]). *Philanthropy, Civil Society, and the State in German History, 1815–1989*. Rochester, NY: Boydell & Brewer.

Adam, T. (2016). *Transnational Philanthropy: The Mond Family's Support for Public Institutions in Western Europe from 1890 to 1938*. Arlington: Palgrave Macmillan.

Anheier, H., & Leat, D. (2006). *Creative Philanthropy: Towards a New Philanthropy for the 21st Century*. London and New York: Routledge.

Azoulay, P., Graff Zivin, J. S., & Manso, G. (2009). *Incentives and Creativity: Evidence from the Academic Life Sciences* (NBER Working Paper No. 15466).

Beveridge, W. (1942). *Social Insurance and Allied Services*. London: HMSO.

Bishop, M., & Green, M. (2008). *Philanthrocapitalism: How the Rich Can Save the World*. New York, NY: Bloomsbury Press.

Blair, K. (2005). Philanthropy for Women's Art in America, Past and Present. In A. Walton (Ed.), *Women and Philanthropy in Education*. Bloomington: Indiana University Press.

Callahan, D. (2017). *The Givers: Wealth, Power, and Philanthropy in a New Gilded Age*. New York: Knopf.

Carnegie, A. (1889). Accessed: https://en.wikisource.org/wiki/The_Gospel_of_ Wealth.

Center for Effective Philanthropy. (2015). *Benchmarking Foundation Governance*. www.effectivephilanthropy.org.

© The Editor(s) (if applicable) and The Author(s), under exclusive license to Springer Nature Switzerland AG 2020
M. Dodgson and D. Gann, *Philanthropy, Innovation and Entrepreneurship*,
https://doi.org/10.1007/978-3-030-38017-5

Charities Aid Foundation. (2016). *Gross Domestic Philanthropy.* https://www. cafonline.org/about-us/blog-home/giving-thought/how-giving-works/ gross-domestic-philanthropy.

Chen, J. (2017). *Clearly.* London: Biteback Books.

Chen, L., Ryan, J., & Saich, A. (2014). Introduction: Philanthropy for Health in China: Distinctive Roots and Future Prospects. In J. Ryan, L. C. Chen, & A. J. Saich (Eds.), *Philanthropy for Health in China.* Bloomington: Indiana University Press.

Collins, C. (2016). *Born on Third Base.* White River Junction, VT: Chelsea Green Publishing.

Coutts Million Pound Donors Report. (2017). *Coutts Million Pound Donors Report 2017.* London: Coutts. https://www.coutts.com/insight-articles/ news/2017/million-pound-donors-report-2017.html.

Crocker, R. (2005). "Nothing More for Men's Colleges": The Educational Philanthropy of Mrs. Russell Sage. In A. Walton (Ed.), *Women and Philanthropy in Education.* Bloomington: Indiana University Press.

De Tocqueville, A. (1835 [2000]). *Democracy in America.* Chicago: University of Chicago Press.

Dodgson, M. (2011). Exploring New Combinations in Innovation and Entrepreneurship: Social Networks, Schumpeter, and the Case of Josiah Wedgwood (1730–1795). *Industrial and Corporate Change, 20*(4), 1119–1151.

Dodgson, M. (2017). Innovation in Firms. *Oxford Review of Economic Policy, 33*(1), 85–100.

Dodgson, M., & Gann, D. (2018). *The Playful Entrepreneur: How to Survive and Thrive in an Uncertain World.* New Haven and London: Yale University Press.

Dodgson, M., Gann, D., & Phillips, N. (Eds.). (2014). *The Oxford Handbook of Innovation Management.* Oxford: Oxford University Press.

Dodgson, M., & Staggs, J. (2012). Government Policy, University Strategy and the Academic Entrepreneur: The Case of Queensland's Smart State Institutes. *Cambridge Journal of Economics, 36*(2), 567–586.

Edwards, M. (2008). *Just Another Emperor? The Myths and Realities of Philanthrocapitalism.* Demos: The Young Foundation.

Freeman, M. (2013). Quakers, Business and Philanthropy. In S. Angell & B. Dandelion (Eds.), *The Oxford Handbook of Quaker Studies.* Oxford: Oxford University Press.

Geddes Poole, A. (2014). *Philanthropy and the Construction of Victorian Women's Citizenship: Lady Frederick Cavendish Miss Emma Cons.* Toronto: University of Toronto Press.

Giridharadas, A. (2018). *Winners Take All: The Elite Charade of Changing the World.* New York: Penguin Random House.

Gramsci, A. (1917, December 24). Philanthropy, Good Will and Organization. *Avanti!*

Jang, H. (2018). Old Money—The History of Giving in Asia. In R. Shapiro, M. Mirchandani, & H. Jang (Eds.), *Pragmatic Philanthropy: Asian Charity Explained*. Singapore: Palgrave Macmillan.

Jaumont, F. (2016). *Unequal Partners: American Foundations and Higher Education Development in Africa*. New York: Palgrave Macmillan.

Jeffreys, E., & Allatson, P. (2015). *Celebrity Philanthropy*. Bristol: Intellect.

Knox, C., & Quirk, P. (2016). *Public Policy, Philanthropy and Peacebuilding in Northern Ireland*. London: Palgrave Macmillan.

Lala, R. (2006). *The Creation of Wealth: The Tatas from the 19th to the 21st Century*. New Delhi: Penguin/Portfolio.

Loebl, S. (2010). *America's Medicis: The Rockefellers and Their Astonishing Cultural Legacy*. New York: Harper.

MacAskill, W. (2017). Effective Altruism: Introduction. *Essays in Philosophy, 18*(1), 1. https://doi.org/10.7710/1526-0569.1580.

Mayer, J. (2016). *Dark Money: How a Secretive Group of Billionaires Is Trying to Buy Political Control in the US*. Melbourne: Scribe Publications.

McClain, M. (2017). *Ellen Browning Scripps: New Money and American Philanthropy*. Lincoln: University of Nebraska.

McGoey, L. (2015). *No Such Thing as a Free Gift*. London: Verso.

Merton, R. (1936). The Unanticipated Consequences of Purposive Social Action. *American Sociological Review, 1*(6), 894–904.

Mulgan, G., Tucker, S., Ali, R., & Sanders, B. (2007). *Social Innovation: What It Is, Why It Matters and How It Can Be Accelerated*. Oxford: Young Foundation/Said Business School.

Murray, F. (2012). *Evaluating the Role of Science Philanthropy in American Research Universities* (NBER Working Paper No. 18146).

Nielson, W. (2002). *Golden Donors*. New Brunswick, NJ: Transaction Publishers.

O'Clery, C. (2007). *The Billionaire Who Wasn't: How Chuck Feeney Secretly Made and Gave Away a Fortune*. New York: Public Affairs.

Offer, A. (1997). Between the Gift and the Market: The Economy of Regard. *Economic History Review, 50*(3), 450–476.

Ostrower, F. (1997). *Why the Wealthy Give: The Culture of Elite Philanthropy*. Princeton, NJ: Princeton University Press.

Perkins, A. (2011). *Edwin Rogers Embree: The Julius Rosenwald Fund, Foundation Philanthropy, and American Race Relations*. Bloomington: Indiana University Press.

Porter, M., & Kramer, M. (2011). Creating Social Value. *Harvard Business Review, 89*(1/2), 62–77.

Prochaska, F. (1990). Philanthropy. In F. Thompson (Ed.), *The Cambridge Social History of Britain* (pp. 1750–1950). Cambridge: Cambridge University Press.

Ramalingam, B., Rush, H., Bessant, J., Marshall, N., Gray, B., Hoffman, K., et al. (2015). *Strengthening the Humanitarian Innovation Ecosystem*. Humanitarian Innovation Ecosystem Research Project Final Report, Brighton University.

Reich, R. (2013, March/April). What Are Foundations For? *Boston Review*.

Reich, R. (2019). *Just Giving: Why Philanthropy Is Failing Democracy and How It Can Do Better*. Princeton, NJ: Princeton University Press.

Reid, A. (2016). Why Is Charitable Activity Tax Protected? In Zinsmeister, K. (2016). How Philanthropy Fuels American Success. In *The Almanac of American Philanthropy*. Washington, DC: Philanthropy Roundtable.

Rittel, H., & Webber, M. (1973). Dilemmas in a General Theory of Planning. *Policy Sciences, 4*(2), 155–169.

Rockefeller, J. (1909 [2013]). *Random Reminiscences of Man and Events*. New York: Creative English Publishers.

Schervish, P. (2003, November 14). *Hyperagency and High-Tech Donors: A New Theory of the New Philanthropists*. New Haven: Boston College Social Welfare Research Institute.

Schneider, W. (2002). *Rockefeller Philanthropy and Modern Biomedicine: International Initiatives from World War I to the Cold War*. Bloomington, IN: Indiana University Press.

Scott, L. (2017). *Private Sector Engagement with Women's Economic Empowerment: Lessons Learned from Years of Practice*. Saïd Business School, University of Oxford.

Seim, D. (2013). *Rockefeller Philanthropy and Modern Social Science*. London: Pickering & Chatto Publishers.

Shapiro, R. (2018). Asian Philanthropy Explained. In R. Shapiro, M. Mirchandani, & H. Jang (Eds.), *Pragmatic Philanthropy: Asian Charity Explained*. Singapore: Palgrave Macmillan.

Shirley, S. (2012). *Let IT Go*. Andrews, UK.

Singer, P. (2015). *The Most Good You Can Do: How Effective Altruism Is Changing Ideas About Living Ethically*. New Haven: Yale University Press.

Skocpol, T. (2016). Politics Symposium: Why Political Scientists Should Study Organized Philanthropy. *PS Political Science and Politics, 49*(3), 433–436.

Sparks, E. (2016). J. Howard Pew. In Zinsmeister, K. (2016). How Philanthropy Fuels American Success. In *The Almanac of American Philanthropy*. Washington, DC: Philanthropy Roundtable.

Tierney, T., & Fleishma, J. (2012). *Give Smart: Philanthropy That Gets Results*. New York: Public Affairs.

Twersky, F. (2014, Summer). The Artful Juggler. *Stanford Social Innovation Review*.

Upchurch, A. (2016). Philanthropists and Policy Advisors. In *The Origins of the Arts Council Movement*. New Directions in Cultural Policy Research. London: Palgrave Macmillan.

Wolf Ditkoff, S., & Grindle, A. (2017, September–October). Audacious Philanthropy. *Harvard Business Review*, pp. 110–118.

Woodruff, P. (2018). *The Ethics of Giving: Philosophers' Perspectives on Philanthropy*. New York: Oxford University Press.

Zinsmeister, K. (2016). How Philanthropy Fuels American Success. In *The Almanac of American Philanthropy*. Washington, DC: Philanthropy Roundtable.

Zunz, O. (2011). *Philanthropy in America: A History*. Princeton University Press: Princeton.

INDEX

© The Editor(s) (if applicable) and The Author(s), under exclusive   117
license to Springer Nature Switzerland AG 2020
M. Dodgson and D. Gann, *Philanthropy,*
Innovation and Entrepreneurship,
https://doi.org/10.1007/978-3-030-38017-5

Printed by Printforce, the Netherlands